FVL
1.00

D0119026

The World's Wild Shores
This first edition copy belongs to

Jerry Welch   Mar 1990

Name   Date

The World's
Wild Shores

FRED WHITEHEAD (ABOVE); GARY BRAASCH (FOLLOWING PAGES)

Warm Atlantic shallows bathe knobbed whelks on the beach of Cumberland Island National Seashore, in Georgia.

FOLLOWING PAGES: In thunderous display, Pacific winter storm waves explode against broken sandstone at Oregon's Shore Acres State Park.

The World's
Wild Shores

Prepared by the Special Publications Division
National Geographic Society, Washington, D.C.

*Hawaiian paradox: Only ten miles
from Kauai's almost rainless coast, 5,148-
foot Mount Waialeale ranks as*

The World's Wild Shores

Contributing Authors
CHRISTINE ECKSTROM, LOREN McINTYRE,
TOM MELHAM, THOMAS O'NEILL,
JENNIFER C. URQUHART

Published by
THE NATIONAL GEOGRAPHIC SOCIETY
GILBERT M. GROSVENOR, *President and
    Chairman of the Board*
MELVIN M. PAYNE, THOMAS W. McKNEW,
    Chairmen Emeritus
OWEN R. ANDERSON, *Executive Vice President*
ROBERT L. BREEDEN, *Senior Vice President,
    Publications and Educational Media*

Prepared by
THE SPECIAL PUBLICATIONS DIVISION
DONALD J. CRUMP, *Director*
PHILIP B. SILCOTT, *Associate Director*
BONNIE S. LAWRENCE, *Assistant Director*

Staff for this Book
MARY ANN HARRELL, *Managing Editor*
JOHN G. AGNONE, *Illustrations Editor*
JODY BOLT, *Art Director*
VICTORIA COOPER, VICTORIA D. GARRETT,
    SUZANNE NAVE PATRICK,
    JACQUELINE N. THOMPSON, *Researchers*
JOHN G. AGNONE, BARBARA BROWNELL,
    RICHARD M. CRUM, ALISON KAHN,
    THOMAS O'NEILL, *Picture Legend Writers*
SUSAN I. FRIEDMAN, *Map Research*
SANDRA F. LOTTERMAN, *Editorial Assistant*
SHARON KOCSIS BERRY, *Illustrations Assistant*

Engraving, Printing, and Product Manufacture
GEORGE W. WHITE, *Director,* and
    VINCENT P. RYAN, *Manager, Manufacturing
    and Quality Management*
DAVID V. SHOWERS, *Production Manager*
KEVIN HEUBUSCH, *Production Project Manager*
LEWIS R. BASSFORD, TIMOTHY H. EWING,
    Assistant Production Managers

CAROL CURTIS, KAREN KATZ, LISA A. LaFURIA,
    JENNIE H. PROCTOR, DRU STANCAMPIANO,
    MARILYN J. WILLIAMS, *Staff Assistants*
DIANE L. COLEMAN, *Indexer*

Copyright © 1990 National Geographic Society
All rights reserved. Reproduction of the whole or any part of
the contents without written permission is prohibited.

Library of Congress CIP Data: page 199

one of the wettest spots on earth— it receives on average 460 inches of rain a year. Among the greenery, *vivid reddish bracts mark the plant called ʻieʻie, akin to pandanus and formerly sacred to hula dancers.*

© FRANS LANTING

Contents

Teeth bared, a northern elephant seal defends

© FRANS LANTING

her newborn pup from western gulls at Año Nuevo Island, off the coast of central California.

Tropical Coasts

Desert Coasts

Warm Temperate Coasts

Cool Temperate Coasts

Polar Coasts

Broadbrush color highlights zones of climate, broadly defined, for the coasts of the world. (Polar takes in subarctic and subantarctic; tropical includes subtropical; desert covers semiarid.) Latitude yields to warm ocean currents in the mild marine climate of western Europe and the Pacific Northwest;

continental climates run to sharper extremes. Tropical seas give moisture to the air; afternoon rains mark the wet tropical weather pattern. Monsoons, seasonal changes in the flow of prevailing winds, determine the wet-and-dry variant. Low-pressure systems deny rain to subtropical deserts, as in the Sahara and the Sinai Peninsula; cold ocean currents help create coastal deserts in Peru, Chile, and Namibia. While the Arctic Ocean tempers the polar chill of the far north, Antarctica's landmass holds an ice cap so huge its melting would raise sea levels and redraw coastlines everywhere.

TROPICAL COASTS:

Shores of Fire and Sun

By Christine Eckstrom

The long evening light of summer in a temperate clime falls upon my table of relics from another world: two rocks, a shell, some black sand, and a pearl. They are souvenirs from the tropics, the belt encircling the earth between the latitudes of Cancer and Capricorn. These lines bound the zone where vertical sunlight can stream down on the tilted, turning earth. The tropics are defined by the sun, which never lingers there at dawn or dusk, or varies much throughout the year. It is a region where I have lived and traveled, in places as scattered as East Africa and Polynesia, the Caribbean and East Asia. Living on an equatorial isle in the Indian Ocean, I would listen at night to the local radio weather report, which could have been prerecorded for most of the world's tropics year in and year out: "Tomorrow, sunny, with afternoon showers likely. Sunrise, 6:18 a.m., sunset 6:18 p.m."

This speaks to the myth of the tropics: as an unchanging world of eternal greenery edged by aquarium seas. My stones and shells tell a different tale. I arrange them on the table in a pattern that suggests a story of the rhythms and seasons of life on tropic shores—of exploding volcanoes and traveling corals, nocturnal primates and migrations of fishes, sea gypsy journeys and the power of mermaids. It evokes a few places, on land and beneath the waves, that fulfill our imaginings of tropic coastal wilds, jeweled with color, eerie with night cries, steamy with decay and new life emerging, like a vision of earth before we began to measure the march of the sun across the sky.

If we were to choose a fountainhead for tropical life, it might be the far-flung archipelagos of southeastern Asia and the western Pacific. Here more than 21,000 islands compose Indonesia, the Philippines, and western Micronesia—

Sea stars' throne, a coral fan brightens Blue Corner, a diving spot for experts in Palau's Rock Islands. Coral reefs ring these Pacific shores.

DAVE B. FLEETHAM / TOM STACK & ASSOCIATES

a chain sprawling along the Equator between the Indian and Pacific Oceans. These islands include the world's second and third largest, New Guinea and Borneo, thick with rain forests and coastal mangroves, and Java with its volcanoes, one of earth's most densely populated lands. At the other extreme are Palau's tiny fairy-castle Rock Islands and its classic coral atoll, a frail ring of green palms and white sand in the lonely ocean. Such a spectrum of environments holds a matching wealth of natural treasures: Indonesia alone has more than 500 species of mammals, at least 1,500 of birds, and perhaps 40,000 species of plants—quite possibly a greater number than the tropics of the Americas or Africa, and 10 percent of all the flora species in the world.

This is a center of earth movements as well. It lies along the hottest spot in the Ring of Fire circling the Pacific, the most active volcanic and seismic zone in the world. Through the ages, as lands here have risen up and subsided, torn apart and rejoined, animals and plants have been marooned and mixed. Coasts have been both an open frontier for arrivals of new species and a closed border for those left behind. Considering this realm of islands, I mapped out a sampling of wild coastal places, some chosen with care and some with fancy, that offer a view of the progression and florescence of tropic life.

For Indonesia, I chose the vicinity of Krakatau, the volcano in the sea between Sumatra and Java that erupted in 1883 in a stupendous explosion. This was by no means the region's worst—that distinction belongs to the eruption of Mount Tambora in 1815, which ranks as the greatest volcanic explosion of the past ten thousand years. Tambora's ash and dust chilled the Northern Hemisphere until Europeans called 1816 "the year without a summer" and New Englanders spoke of "1800-and-froze-to-death." Even so, Krakatau's outburst was devastating, and much better documented than its predecessors.

Krakatau blasted out five cubic miles of debris—20 times more than Mount St. Helens ejected in 1980—and sent up a cloud of gas and ash 30 miles high. Pressure waves in the atmosphere affected tide gauges as far away as Panama and France. Booms "like the distant roars of heavy guns" were heard almost 3,000 miles west; off Sumatra, a British sea captain reported that "the eardrums of over half my crew have been shattered." Ocean waves traveling 350 miles per hour crashed ashore on nearby isles as tsunami 100 feet high, sweeping entire towns out to sea. Floating pumice clogged the seas; one vessel in the Indian Ocean steamed through "a vast field of pumice" for 1,250 miles. Most of a volcano 2,600 feet high was adrift in earth's oceans and skies; a telegram from Java just after the explosion said simply, "Where once Mount Krakatau stood the sea now plays."

Because local destruction of plant and animal life was so apocalyptic, the remains of the volcano—a high, half-moon isle now known as Rakata—gave scientists an opportunity to study the recolonization of an empty tropic shore. From "one microscopic spider—only one," observed in 1884, life returned in a nearly evolutionary progression, carried on currents of wind and sea. First came algae, mosses, and ferns, then grasses and conifers, followed by orchids, flowering shrubs, and deciduous trees. Migratory birds paid visits; animal settlers came in sequence—insects, lizards, crocodiles, and land birds. One mammal, the rat, appeared later. Then, in 1927, the seas by Rakata started to bubble.

My two cherished rocks—one basalt, black and dense; one pumice, gray-white and sponge-light—came from the summit and the beach of Anak Krakatau (Child of Krakatau), the volcano that has risen since 1927 as a new companion to Rakata. If Rakata's shores are a place to contemplate the rise of tropic life, then Anak Krakatau is a place to imagine the beginning of the earth.

With photographer Paul Chesley, I arrived aboard the ketch *Capella Star,* to explore the volcano whose very name sounds like an explosion and to see what life has gained a foothold on its shores. Among early visitors were huge seagoing snakes that swam across from Sumatra, fat reticulated pythons that can grow 30 feet long. I scanned the strait for them—in vain—but my eyes kept returning to the pale plume of smoke ahead. The volcano has the magnetic allure of horror; someday it will erupt again.

We sailed in silence between Rakata and Anak Krakatau. An assortment of debris floated past—pumice, branches, seed pods—like tokens of death and rebirth. On one flank of Anak Krakatau, waves exploded in sprays of white foam against tumbled black boulders; on another, fissures steamed. Rounding a high dune of black sand, we anchored off a narrow beach backed by casuarinas, in sight of the volcano's plume.

It was dusk, and Paul and I hiked up the dune for a view of the peak. At the crest, where the gusty wind smelled of sulfur, we planned a route to the top for the morning. To the west, the ragged profile of Sumatra etched the sky. Mountains of cumulus, orange in sunset, circled the horizon like airborne volcanoes. We descended in darkness, bats swooping overhead, our way faintly lit by heat lightning. On a moonless night, the skies strobing with white light, we felt transported to earliest time. I imagined a volcano cooled, then green with forests, its slopes drained by streams where air-breathing fishes could venture ashore. Over long millennia those ancient lungfishes gave rise to amphibians and reptiles—and they to birds and mammals; I wondered what might evolve in future from the little fish called mudskippers that creep onto land in the coastal mangrove swamps of the Pacific today.

At dawn we climbed the volcano to the very plume, where hot, gauzy vapors swirled around us, some sulfurous, some smelling like a public bath. They came steaming up from cracks and spongy soft spots on a surface caked yellow and white with sulfur and salts. We felt a bit like madmen tempting the earth to convert us, in one mighty blast, back to primordial gases.

With a peculiar sense of accomplishment, we returned to the beach—now griddle-hot in the sun—and took a swim. Floating in gentle waves, I listened to the music of birds on shore and the whistle of the wind in the casuarinas. Purple beach morning glories, whose long seed pods I had seen in the sea, blossomed along the beach. Schools of fish leaped near me in low splashing arcs. The air smelled like sea spray and pines, and I was lulled into forgetful peace. Standing up, I burrowed my toes into the sand—and struck an underwater heat vent that nearly burned my feet, a spell-breaking reminder that I was on the shores of a tropic isle still in creation.

Krakatau is one hot link in a chain of volcanoes extending through Sumatra and Java and east to Bali. This marks a boundary between tectonic plates, the huge slabs of earth's crust that slowly shift over the molten interior. In the archipelagos of Indonesia and the Philippines, crustal plates have separated, collided, and dived under one another—and continue to do so. When sea levels were low during the ice ages, land bridges connected the westerly isles to the Asian mainland, creating a great curved peninsula, while New Guinea and the isles around it formed part of Australia. In the heart of the East Indies, deep seas surround Sulawesi (formerly known as Celebes), which may never have been linked to other isles or continents.

*L*ong before scientists formulated the theory of continental drift, a naturalist named Alfred Russel Wallace, who worked in the East Indies during the 1850s and '60s, found evidence of an invisible line separating the eastern and western isles. He discovered it by studying wildlife, often traveling on foot through trackless forests and by boat to remote shores. He collected scores of new species, and, independently, came to the same conclusions that Charles Darwin had reached about the rise of life on earth. Life-forms are not necessarily permanent, he decided: "change of species, still more of generic and of family form, is a matter of time." He sent his ideas to Darwin in a letter that prompted Darwin to put his own thoughts on paper and publish them; his essay appeared, with Wallace's, in 1858.

History—and geography—have preserved Wallace's name for another discovery. He gradually realized a remarkable fact: that the fauna of the westerly isles was primarily Asian, while that of the eastern islands resembled Australia's. The distinction is most startling with the birds of Bali and Lombok, neighboring isles. Bali's birds are Asian; Lombok's, Australian. "The strait is here fifteen miles wide," he wrote in his classic book *The Malay Archipelago*, "so that we may pass in two hours from one great division of the earth to another. . . ."

Wallace drew a zoological boundary between the isles of the region, one now recognized as a major zoogeographic division and called, appropriately, Wallace's Line. It roughly corresponds with a geological line between the Indian and Pacific Ocean plates, and with the Ice Age limits of the Asian continental shelf. It's a boundary between species in sight of each other's shores.

Aside from the birds of Bali and Lombok, Wallace's strongest evidence came from mammals. Those of the western isles are Asian, placentals; those of the eastern isles are Australian, marsupials. Their distribution suggests that it was islands and sea levels—not the mammals—that moved. Since his time, scientists have proposed adjustments to Wallace's original line and added new boundaries, because of an assortment of anomalies and, in part, the varied mammals of Sulawesi. This island has both placentals and marsupials. Some biogeographers now draw two Wallace's lines, to the east and west of Sulawesi, and they name the zone between them Wallacea.

Sulawesi is shaped like a sprawling four-armed octopus. Ranges of mountains and volcanoes along the arms isolate distinct environments; each arm, for instance, has its own species of tailless macaque. One particular area on the tip of the northern arm lured me in the footsteps of Wallace.

Today the Tangkoko-Batuangus Dua Saudara Reserve covers about 34 square miles of wild land, from the black sand beaches and coastal rain forests around the village of Batuputih up to the damp moss forests around the top of a volcano. Wallace spent more than a week on this coast in 1859 to collect the rare *maleo* fowl. These handsome black-and-white birds don't use body heat to incubate their eggs. In the interior, the females lay and bury their eggs near hot springs or volcanic vents. During the dry months, May through September, some visit the sand beaches to lay the clutch above highwater mark. I came in a wetter season, to visit the rain forest that shelters both Asian and Australian mammals.

Next to my rocks from Krakatau, the cup of black sand, coarse like broken peppercorns, comes from the beach south of Batuputih, where I camped in a bungalow one night before heading out to search for two mammals of Wallacea—the bigeyed tarsier, *Tarsius spectrum,* a tiny Asian primate; and a furry marsupial known as the cuscus. That night I slept with a large machete under the bed, lent by rangers who insisted that I have a weapon handy "in case something happens with the wild animals." I suppose that some snakes and the wild babirusa pig can be dangerous, but I was lulled by the night sounds of the forests—the great crescendos and staccatos of screeching insects, the gulping squeaks of geckos racing around the ceiling, the cries of unknown creatures high up, far off, and the rhythmic boom of the surf, a skipping stone's throw from the door.

Just before dawn, a small party came to lead me into the forest: the chief ranger, Wodi Tulende, ranger Jenley Gawina, and my guide, Boy Sumual. Even at 5 a.m., the air was so humid that trees dripped. Damp leaves underfoot muffled our steps as we followed a narrow path within sound of the sea. A few minutes down the trail, Wodi paused. A high chorus of light whooping songs—delicate, like the music of small birds—sounded in the trees ahead. Wodi cocked his head to listen, his eyes wide, and whispered, *"Tarsius."*

The music stopped as we approached; no leaves rustled. Wodi stared at a ficus tree arching over the trail. He bent near it and sniffed, looked up and nodded, then sniffed higher up a bough, slowly raising his eyes to where the ficus leaned against an old tree with a small hole in its trunk. When he shone his flashlight at the hollow, two golden eyes gleamed. *"Tarsius,"* he repeated.

We watched, motionless. After a while, the tarsier slipped out to hide among the leaves and peek down. I stared, transfixed, at the huge round eyes of a fellow primate the size of my fist, as he stared back at me.

With eyes 150 times larger in relation to body size than are human eyes, the tarsier is well adapted to a nocturnal life. So, presumably, were the earliest mammals, which appeared during the dinosaur age. Warm blood—stability of body heat—enabled them to be active in the chilly hours of darkness, while a planet of cold-blooded reptiles rested. For mammals, the first successful niche may have been the night.

A mere 50 yards farther, we spotted the other mammal I had hoped to see. High in a willowy tree sat a family of cuscus, an adult male and female and a juvenile, gazing at us with eyes blinking in the sunrise light. These particular marsupials are as big as raccoons, have an opposable "thumb" on each hind foot, and resemble a furry brown opossum with a few stray bear genes. These traits inspired their scientific name, *Phalanger ursinus*—*Phalanger* for the distinctive toe, *ursinus* for the bear look.

They must fear little; they move like sloths, coiling their long tails around the branches, hanging upside down, and reaching up in slow motion to grasp the trunk and inch upright. The adult female had moved higher up the tree when we first appeared, staying motionless there, and we understood her caution when a tiny head poked up from her pouch.

Even though the forest edged the sea, where salt waves and spray affect survival, it seemed as if no two trees were alike. There are so many species in the tropical rain forest that new ones are constantly being discovered. An expedition of entomologists found at least 100 new species of insects at Tangkoko in 1985—and are still analyzing their finds. Wodi, who has assisted researchers of every nationality, seemed to know the name of everything in the forest—in Latin, the naturalist's lingua franca. But when I asked him what kind of tree our tarsier lived in, he explained that no one knew; its leaves had recently been sent to Jakarta for identification. Because of this floral richness, the tarsier need not go far to find what he needs to survive; in fact, his home range is only about 25 square feet. The tarsier and the cuscus, although neighbors, may never cross paths on Tangkoko's forested shore.

We are the land mammals that ventured across the seas. Apparently people from southeast Asia first entered Indonesia and the Philippines when Ice Age sea levels left this area a great peninsula. Then, perhaps as early as 2000 to 6000 B.C., people set off to sea in outrigger canoes, exploring and colonizing islands of the Pacific and west as far as Madagascar. Their navigational feats stand unrivaled, suggesting the sophistication of their knowledge of stars, winds, currents—and of seas and shores they explored and settled.

Near my black sand from Tangkoko, I have placed a small pearl, a natural white one, oblong and imperfect. It's a reminder of the people known as the Bajau, sea gypsies of the Philippines. Traditionally they have lived in houseboats, along the shore at Zamboanga, a town at the southwestern tip of Mindanao, and in the long chain of islands that once formed part of the Ice Age peninsula. Their expert knowledge of tides and currents and sea creatures let them follow the movements of fish, and they would trade part of their catch for rice and fruit and vegetables grown by land dwellers. Today most of them belong to households on shore, but still rely on small houseboats for fishing trips. Outsiders tell fabulous stories about their skills. They can stay underwater longer than ordinary mortals, it's said, and can even communicate with fish.

Directly in front of the small hotel where I stayed in Zamboanga, dozens of outriggers, known locally as *vintas*, rocked in the shallows. Two guides from the Department of Tourism, Mario Matias and Ignacio Sanico, told me about their Bajau owners. Instead of roaming between moorages, said Mario, they stay in Zamboanga, and they sell pearls and shells. He spoke admiringly of their knowledge of sea and sky. "They are better than the weather bureau. They know when a typhoon is coming. When you can't see their boats here, it is fine weather—they are fishing. They use no compass, no lights. They know the stars. They are not astronomers, but they can tell you where you are."

This knowledge, Ignacio added, includes folklore heavily tinged with the supernatural. "They watch everything for signs. The sun, the stars, the animals."

On the narrow beach, Ignacio introduced me to a Bajau named Ningning Gallos, who harvests seaweed and dives for corals to sell—but not for pearls any more. "Too deep!" he said, shaking his head. He was born on a vinta, has lived by this beach all his life, and has recently married. During the calm dry season from January to May, he and his wife live on the vinta; but in the rough rainy weather of the southwest monsoon, from June to December, he sometimes stays in a small stilt house perched over the water near shore. (Such houses have long been the homes of shore dwellers known as the Samal folk.)

Ignacio translated Ningning's explanations to me when I asked about weather signs and sea creatures. Most of the latter seemed to connote luck, and each animal I mentioned had a fantastical tale: "Sea snakes are 99 percent luck. If you can catch one and keep it alive in the sea until it dies a natural death, the snake will turn into a metal, like bronze, and it will give you power, like a magician.

"If you are good, then you may be lucky enough to find a dolphin. We seldom see them here, and if you do, you can make a wish on him, like a star."

When Ignacio asked Ningning to tell me the most unusual thing he had ever seen in the sea, he replied, "A turtle." Sea turtles have been overhunted and their eggs overharvested in the Philippines, as elsewhere. According to Ningning, if you are lucky, you may find a nest of turtle eggs on the beach, and if you are given the power of luck, the eggs will become pearls in your hands.

"I also asked if he has ever seen a mermaid," Ignacio volunteered. "But he says he has never seen one."

"Has anyone seen a mermaid?" I asked Ignacio.

"I'm not sure," he replied, "but last October there was talk that this hotel was holding a mermaid, because there was a big typhoon, with heavy rains and gusty winds, that lasted many days, and the people said that somebody must be keeping a mermaid, and that's why the typhoon would not stop. They were saying, 'Release the mermaid! Release the mermaid so the rain will stop!' They even announced on the radio that there was a mermaid here, and people flocked to this hotel to see her. They came from far away, many on foot; they even wanted to pay an entrance fee of 50 pesos, which is a lot for the people here. There were so many people gathered outside that the guests could not pass in and out. After a week, the typhoon finally stopped, and the people said, 'They released the mermaid.' But if another storm comes, I am sure the people will say, 'The mermaid is back.'"

Due west of Zamboanga lies the Philippine isle of Palawan. Paul Chesley and I traveled to a cluster of isles north of it, an area renowned for sheer physical beauty and known as El Nido. Made of cracked black marble and ancient coral limestone, these isles look like gigantic cathedrals afloat in the sea, spired with jagged pinnacles, trimmed with tiny crescents of white sand and groves of palms and pandanus—a holiday poster of paradise.

In a motor-outrigger known as a pumpboat, Paul and I explored the isles one day, watching for nesting sea turtles and for the tiny swiftlet that gave the area its name. (Literally, in Spanish *el nido* means "the nest"; locally it refers to the bird and its preferred habitat as well.) We cruised through great amphitheaters of sea, rimmed by isles with impossible shapes—great crowns and tiaras, organ pipes and hobbit castles, raggedy sea monsters and great breaching whales. Tenny Genovaña, born and brought up here, accompanied us and told us about the seasons of life around the isles.

It was early April, Philippine summer, and nearing the end of the six-month dry season. "In the sea this is the season of squid," Tenny explained. "The fishermen go out to catch them with hand lines, from the sunset into the night." It was the tuna season too, when schools of yellow fin come down from Japan, heading south. "Also, it is anchovy season. The tuna come to the surface to catch them. We use a net and a light for the anchovy at night, and troll for tuna all day. The whales come through in the month of May," he added. "The sea is calm then, and you can see them blowing. The people come just to watch them pass by."

On land it was the season of cashews, "the season to make money" according to Tenny, and for the swiftlets it was the season for making their nests. At one small isle we watched the local hunters, suspended on ropes from steep cliffs above a sea of high slapping swells. They were collecting nests that are, incredibly, made of the birds' saliva and command a caviar price for use in el nido soup. Here, as in China, this soup is a great delicacy. "They collect the nests every 15 days," Tenny told us, "but not in May. That is the season of eggs. In June, when the chicks can fly, the collectors can come back again."

Once we did spot three fresh sea turtle tracks—probably from hawksbills, which nest off and on through the year—leading up a white beach. Two men peeked out at us from behind massive rocks, and we chose not to go ashore. Most likely, we were told later, the turtles had been killed and the eggs collected for sale. As an aficionado of sea turtles, in part for the mysterious power of their migration instinct and in part for the wondrous persistence of their ancient form, I could hardly hope that those eggs turned to pearls.

As ancient voyagers traveled eastward, they settled isles that were progressively smaller and more widely scattered. The farther from the mainland, the fewer species these islands held. Often the voyagers carried cargoes of food plants and domestic animals, but even so their survival depended on the sea.

The last memento on my table is the shell of a young giant clam from the Palau group, the westernmost isles of Micronesia. Palauans have lived here so long that at least one of their creation legends is not a tale of an ancient voyage. I came across a story that the islands and the people were born from the sea, and sprang forth from a giant clam.

Palauans recognize seasons for every stage in the life cycles of their islands' plants, birds, and sea life—especially the fish. The men are famed as fishermen, and fishing skills are cultivated as a point of honor; good fishermen enjoy prestige quite apart from their inherited standing in society. What in times past ensured survival has been raised to a sign of rank, an indicator of dependence on the sea.

When I arrived there in April, it was six days after the new moon, the time when *meas*, or rabbit fish—a local favorite—head out from the mangroves to spawn on the reefs. With Palauan fisherman and diver Francis Toribiong, I watched men hunting fish in the shallows near a reef. They were spaced far apart, working in prescribed areas designated according to their rank. With cast nets slung over the shoulders, they stalked the waters like herons. Spotting a school, they ever so slowly readied their nets and tossed them out in white spinning disks. Despite their patience and skill, only about half of them were successful enough to smile as they returned.

In the southern isles of Palau, people recognize another kind of season—one of drifting logs. These logs are carried out to their isles on certain annual currents from Indonesia, after the rains there have swept fallen trees into the sea. I imagine that, a century ago, after the eruption of Krakatau, there must have been a season of floating pumice—at least for a while.

Like biological hitchhikers, some plants and animals have colonized remote islands by drifting ashore on logs and debris. In the wake of Krakatau's explosion, scientists found that rafts of floating pumice not only carried land plants and animals to distant shores, but also sheltered a melange of sea life—some attached, like barnacles; some merely following along, like certain fishes. Recently marine scientists have demonstrated that corals, too, can travel to faraway places and establish new colonies there after attaching themselves to rafts of pumice. Such a link between the volcanoes and corals suggests an intriguing possibility. The isles of east Asia, which currently make up the most active volcanic zone in the world, and are the home to more species of coral than any other place on earth, may be a fountainhead for tropic life undersea as well as on land.

With Francis Toribiong, I set out to experience the wonder of the underwater coral world for which Palau is famous. We zipped off in a motorboat through the Rock Islands, emerald mushroom-shaped isles aswirl with white-tailed tropicbirds. We sped along 20 miles south to a dark violet patch in the turquoise seas just north of the island of Peleliu. There we anchored to dive the dark patch, a blue hole in the reef.

Through depths of ever-darkening blues we swam 100 feet down a vertical shaft in the coral. We came to a side hole, like a secret passage, that led out and up to a wildly colorful reef, flickering with fish. There were tiny reef fish in outlandish patterns and pulsing hues; schools of yellow, blue, and silvery snappers; grouper, barracuda, and napoleon fish—and three gray reef sharks, slowly cruising. I felt as if I were inside a three-dimensional Jackson Pollock painting as it was being created with splashes and splatters, or inside a turning kaleidoscope where the chips of color changed to fish and aligned themselves into fast-streaming schools. I swam along beside a hawksbill turtle for a while, before it put on a burst of speed and vanished into the blue distance. Then, slowly ascending from a kingdom of life that survives only in the warmth of tropic seas, I surfaced to a view of a white beach and a wild green shore—a sight that, over eons of time, has met the eyes of uncounted creatures just emerged from the sea.

FOLLOWING PAGES: A nine-foot Komodo dragon charges an intruder. World's largest lizards, these inhabit four of Indonesia's Lesser Sunda Islands.

© 1985 JOSÉ AZEL / CONTACT PRESS IMAGES

Hardy pioneer, beach morning glory colonizes a beach of volcanic cinders and ash at Indonesia's Anak Krakatau, "child of Krakatau." In 1883 the parent volcano exploded, obliterating life for miles around and leaving a great caldera. Slowly, seeds and insects borne on wind or wave revived the wasteland.

Then, in 1927, Anak Krakatau began emerging from the sea-flooded crater. It erupts almost yearly, causing local devastation but opening new frontiers for living creatures—and for science. At right, wild cane rooted in the ash of a 1988 explosion waves on a slope of the young cinder cone.

PAUL CHESLEY / PHOTOGRAPHERS ASPEN (BOTH)

23

PAUL CHESLEY / PHOTOGRAPHERS ASPEN

In the wake of Anak Krakatau's 1988 activity , a young visitor examines the material it ejected. Vents spew

sulfur and other gases that turn debris
yellow and white. Nearby, Rakata—
remnant of Krakatau—looms silently.

Its plume, not steam but a placid cloud,
forms as warm moist air flows upslope
to the cooler elevation of the summit.

*Life-forms define frontiers in the islands
of Indonesia. On Sulawesi, the Tangkoko
Reserve (below) shelters the tiny primate
called a tarsier (opposite) and other
examples of Southeast Asian mammals.
It also holds marsupials very like
Australia's. Elsewhere, straits sever
these two faunas. Studying regional
quirks of distribution in the 1850s,
the naturalist Alfred Russel Wallace
developed a theory of evolution similar
to that of his friend Charles Darwin.*

PAUL CHESLEY / PHOTOGRAPHERS ASPEN (BOTH); MICHAEL S. YAMASHITA (FOLLOWING PAGES)

*FOLLOWING PAGES: Youngsters frolic
on a surf beach in southeastern Bali,
where storm and sea sculpt the coast.*

"Sea gypsies"—so the Samal folk of Mindanao, in the Philippines, call themselves. But they live ashore as professed Muslims, like village elder Latip Hussin and his wife (opposite). Residence and religion once separated them from a related people, the Bajau. Pagans who spent their lives on small houseboats, the Bajau roamed the sea, fishing and selling their catch. Now many Bajau have adopted Islam and settled in villages built on stilts. Below, Samal vintas, *dugouts used for fishing, head to sea under bright sails brought out on days of ceremony.*

PAUL CHESLEY / PHOTOGRAPHERS ASPEN (BOTH AND FOLLOWING PAGES)

FOLLOWING PAGES: At an area called El Nido, the author tests Palawan waters; a motorized "pumpboat" stands by.

© DAVID DOUBILET (BOTH)

*On a reef in the Bismarck Sea, east of
New Guinea, a local fisherman dives
for a giant clam, a popular food item.
Reefs hereabouts teem with some 2,000
species of fish. A tiny goby
(above, left) blends with red coral;
it can vary its color for camouflage,
protection against predators.*

PAUL CHESLEY / PHOTOGRAPHERS ASPEN (FOLLOWING PAGES)

FOLLOWING PAGES: *The Rock Islands—*
200-odd ancient coral reefs, formed on
extinct volcanoes—mark a spacious
lagoon in the Palau group.

TROPICAL COASTS:

A Portfolio

Straddling the Equator between the Tropics of Capricorn and Cancer, the tropical climate zone rules nearly a third of the world's coastlines. Here the sun rides high overhead year-round, and temperatures normally range from warm to hot. Rainfall defines two subtypes of climate: tropical wet, the most predictable of all; and tropical wet and dry, a variant that allows a dry season.

To about ten degrees north or south of the Equator, tropical wet prevails. Moisture-laden trade winds from north and south converge here, providing almost daily showers and rarely revving up to gale force.

Beyond ten degrees north and south, tropical storms may ravage coastal areas. These notorious rotating storms—hurricanes, typhoons, or cyclones—always develop over water. They usually form in summer and autumn, when waters are warmest; and often, but not always, they follow familiar tracks. Typhoons moving westward from the Marianas have often battered Philippine shores with wind, waves, and as much as 17 inches of rain in a day.

Prevailing wind patterns also create surface currents that circulate the sun-drenched tropic waters, earth's warmest. Such waters sustain myriad species of marine life, including the reef-building corals that may themselves become shores. And upon the coasts, moist warm conditions foster about half the world's species of plants and animals—including some that promote disease. "Pesthole" was once as much a cliché of the tropics as "paradise" is now.

Yet the peoples of tropical coasts have enjoyed the bounty of land and sea, and to this day seafarers of the old school—in Polynesia, the Philippines, Brazil—rely on their consistent climate to sail as their ancestors did, without compasses or charts. By reading clouds, currents, and ocean swells, they traverse their wild shores in traditional craft, with timeless confidence.

*B*uilding raw new shore for the Big Island, *Hawaii, lava from erupting Kilauea pours into the Pacific under a billowing column of steam.*

RON WATTS / FIRST LIGHT

*M*olded by gentle currents, a sandbar forms in northern reaches of the Great Barrier Reef,

PAUL CHESLEY / PHOTOGRAPHERS ASPEN

earth's longest. It runs 1,250 miles along Australia's northeastern coast.

CAROL HUGHES (BOTH)

Sunset brings sea turtles ashore to nest. Thousands of olive ridley females crowd Nancite Beach, on Costa Rica's northwest coast, during the arribada—arrival en masse. Riding Pacific currents, they begin to gather offshore in July. By October, nearly 100,000 strong, they converge on a beach. Smallest and lightest of their kind—with shell length of two feet or less, and weighing at most 100 pounds—they leave the faintest of trails. They dig nests in the sand, lay about 100 eggs apiece, then return wearily to sea. Below, black vultures escort potential prey. The olive or Pacific ridley is one of eight sea turtle species—all dependent on sand beaches for survival.

A magnificent frigatebird takes a two-inch ridley hatchling that had escaped other birds and ghost crabs on its first journey to the sea— a sortie by instinct after 60 days'

GARY BRAASCH (BELOW); DAVID HUGHES (LEFT)

incubation. Of the thousands of sea turtles hatched in an arribada, only a few survive. At right, above, baby leatherbacks—unmolested and lucky—struggle across hard, damp sand of a Pacific beach in Costa Rica. Leatherbacks seem to range farther than other species, but all adults mate at sea. Then females return to their coastal nesting sites.

On Brazil's northeast coast, a
fisherman launches his jangada, or
raft of buoyant logs. Indians
called the tricorn sail a "white

46

LOREN McINTYRE

*tongue." Prevailing winds and
currents power and guide these craft.*

*V*olcanic cliffs of northern Molokai evoke a dark history: In the 1800s Hawaiian lepers endured

RICHARD ALEXANDER COOKE III

banishment nearby. Now a hospital offers prime care to patients who leave at will.

M olokai's beaches offer tranquillity to a population one-third native Hawaiian by descent.

This grandfather and grandson share a mellow tradition—an evening fishing trip.

RICHARD ALEXANDER COOKE III

51

WARM TEMPERATE COASTS:

Storms and Sanctuaries

By Thomas O'Neill

Whoever has felt the sting of blowing sand or heard the roar and seen the concussion of high waves crashing onto a beach knows that all coasts are inherently wild. The shoreline may seem pacified with ocean-view hotels, houses moored in dune grass, and seawalls as thick as fortress gates, but it's a deception. The sea strips away all illusions of permanence. Unpredictable and powerful, the oceans of the world assure that no coastline—built-up or left in its natural state—is ever tamed. Towering waves born of a storm far away, a brush with a hurricane, or just abnormally high tides and sharp winds can turn any Oceanfront Drive into Desolation Row.

Such destruction occurred in March 1989 along the low sandy mid-Atlantic coastline of the United States. A northeaster with gale-force winds hammered at land's edge for four days. Storm waves smashed into the Outer Banks of North Carolina like runaway freight trains, uprooting homes, snapping off the ends of fishing piers, smothering buildings in sand. Eyewitnesses described motel rooms floating out to sea. In Maryland, millions of cubic yards of sand were wiped off resort beaches.

I took special notice of this storm for what it did *not* do to a reach of wilderness shore. In the midst of wreckage, one area was spared: a group of barrier islands off the Virginia coast. Here one observer reported, "Well, a lot of sand was moved around; that was it."

With a few exceptions, the Virginia islands have no oceanfront development to suffer a storm's wrath. Largely uninhabited, they have been given back to beach, dunes, grasslands, forest, and marsh. They have been set aside as the Virginia Coast Reserve, a wilderness sanctuary that includes all or part of 13

*Beginning its food quest on a November evening,
a whitetail buck passes the salt marsh on the
western shore of Georgia's Cumberland Island.*

FRED WHITEHEAD

barrier islands stretching 51 miles along the Delmarva Peninsula. Because they represent an undisturbed system, I chose them as one of three areas where I could enjoy the satisfactions of a wild subtropical coast: viewing high, wind-swept dune lines, walking broad beaches loaded with shells, boating through labyrinthian marshlands, watching wildlife.

The second lies in the sea islands off Georgia. This is Cumberland Island, which offers a magnificent beach 16 miles long, a moss-hung live oak forest straight from a southern gothic novel, and a hard-won status as a national seashore. I found the third across the Atlantic, on the southwestern coast of Spain. Here Doñana National Park preserves a landscape celebrated for its towering African-style dunes, its wetlands, its mammals, and its value as one of Europe's richest nesting and feeding grounds for shorebirds and waterfowl.

As wilderness coasts, the three have much in common. All existed once as aristocratic getaways and hunting grounds. All gained their wilderness status in the past 20 years, and all survive as sanctuaries on densely populated vacation coasts. Scientists and naturalists are busy at all three, studying still-intact ecosystems. And finally, with the ceaseless advance of wind and wave, these three wild coasts share a state of constant transformation quite aside from storms like that March northeaster.

"Most of these islands are as flat as pancakes, and during that storm the beaches went underwater, the storm energy rolled over the islands, and the next day *our* beaches were back." Barry Truitt, manager of the Virginia Coast Reserve, was talking about his islands as though they were prizewinning gymnasts who had effortlessly completed a difficult maneuver. A twangy Virginia native, he works for the Nature Conservancy, a new-breed environmental group that uses private monies to buy land and protect habitat for plants and animals. It had purchased the Virginia islands at bargain prices—an average of $200 an acre—between 1967 and 1975.

Oceanfront today is often just another word for prime real estate. Buildings, roads, and seawalls materialize practically at the high-tide line. Mile after mile of shore in the developed world now looks almost identical, with great balconied palisades of condominiums and high-rise hotels. Their built-up beaches are shrinking, however, eroding as storm waves, lacking space to discharge their energy, wash away the sand. Resorts like Ocean City and Miami Beach now spend millions of dollars to have sand pumped back onto their dwindling strands, while wild beaches renew themselves. "Leave a beach alone and it will always be there," Barry Truitt told me. "Maybe it won't be in the same spot, but I guarantee it will be there."

A beach was changing before my eyes one raw February morning when I explored Hog Island in Barry's domain. Frozen *Spartina* grass in the high marsh crunched under my boots, and a northwest wind howled so loudly I could barely hear the surf. Often it is the off-seasons that reveal a coast at its wildest and most dynamic. Partisans of wilderness shores may consider summer an anticlimax: the weather largely unchanging, beaches packed with sunbathers, the inland swarming with mosquitoes and flies and ticks and chiggers, and the large flocks of migratory birds away on migration.

February it was. My face burned from the wind as I turned south down the seven-mile strand. The beach was anything but empty. Legions of sanderlings—little shorebirds that move with the alacrity of wind-up toys—scampered across the swash zone, hunting for tiny mollusks and crustaceans in the wet sand before the next wave could roll in. Farther on, several hundred snow geese had taken a break from grazing on the marshes and congregated on the sand, as thick as Coney Island bathers. The large white birds squawked and murmured among themselves, allowing me to get quite close before lifting off like an explosion of confetti. Two or three thousand of them winter in the vicinity. In another month they would start north to the Arctic to breed. Later they would be replaced by other migrants—snowy egrets, night herons, glossy ibis—that nest in the thickets and return south for the winter.

In early summer these same beaches would be jammed with other birds, notably whimbrels, dunlins, and sandpipers. Shorebirds such as oystercatchers and piping plovers nest on the open sand, as do colonies of terns, gulls, and black skimmers. As I walked along, trying to imagine the scene, a peregrine falcon suddenly hurtled out across the grassy dunes and cruised over the breakers, hunting. The sanderlings, its favored prey, scattered like leaves.

At my feet the beach was seething. Rivulets of sand, pushed by the strong wind, were streaming across it like pulses of energy. Wherever the sand collided with an obstacle—a shell, a clump of beach grass, my boots—it started to heap up in little dunes. I could practically feel the beach expanding as sand poured across it. Here on the northern end of Hog, the beach had grown so fast in recent years that it had left the dune fields far behind. In the words of coastal geologists, Hog is rotating, accreting on the upper end and eroding on the lower. In the past half-century the northern end has quadrupled in width, from a few hundred yards wide to three-quarters of a mile.

Moreover, the islands are not only building up and slimming down, but also *moving*, migrating westward toward the shore as mean sea level rises. Individual islands are literally rolling over themselves as dunes override marsh and marsh in turn takes over mud flats. In 1987 a scientific team began a five-year study of the Virginia barrier system, sponsored by the National Science Foundation. The specialists and their assistants make their headquarters at a restored farmhouse near the town of Oyster, and there one foggy winter day I called on Raymond D. Dueser, director of the Long-Term Ecological Research program. Rising from his laptop computer, Dr. Dueser gestured toward the shrouded water and said that "out there" scientists can come as close as they ever will to instant gratification. Significant changes in most natural systems, he explained, usually take much longer than the human life span. "But here we can watch them happen."

Study of core samples and historical photographs will detail the environmental history of the islands; a computer simulation model will predict future changes. Fieldwork will delve into marsh productivity, plant succession, terrestrial and marine food chains, nutrient cycling, and storm effects. Dr. Dueser was impatient to install a monitoring system to be ready for a big blow.

"We are overdue for a hurricane," he said. "The last extreme event was the Ash Wednesday Storm of 1962 when many of the islands went under. Since then they've been developing full-tilt boogie, as fast as a barrier island system can go. How long will our luck hold out?" (It held through September 1989, when Hurricane Hugo spared this area.)

In grave tones, Dr. Dueser went on to discuss the "greenhouse effect." If the global climate continues to heat up and the melting of polar ice quickens, the rise in sea level will accelerate drastically—from an average of four inches a century to, in worst-case projections, nine feet per century. "If that happens we will be in place to study the effects on the coastline," he stressed. "Remember, two-thirds of the world's population lives in the coastal zone. The impact of even a two-foot rise could be immense."

It was low water that worried Barry Truitt the morning he took me out to visit Parramore Island. We left on a rising tide, but in shallow Hog Island Bay the boat was almost thumping bottom in places. We made our way cautiously, scaring up large flocks of brant and black duck but hardly attracting a glance from a few hardy folks out picking oysters.

About eight miles out, Barry turned up a "gut," the local name for a tidal creek, and steered along Revel Island. Four raccoons were creeping around the roof of a dilapidated hunting lodge, probably licking up dew for their freshwater ration. Exclusive hunting clubs enjoyed the area in the late 19th and early 20th centuries, when a single blast of a shotgun could fell dozens of birds. President Grover Cleveland was a guest of that era, which eventually came to an end under the blows of northeasters, hurricanes, and the Great Depression.

Our weather was passive—bright and calm—when Barry docked at Parramore Island. Hiking to the beach, we had to skirt soggy marshlands. Barry halted several times to exercise his hunter's vision, calling out the names of the various ducks on nearby ponds: buffleheads, gadwalls, pintails, mallards, black ducks. A path led us through thickets of cat briar and past Italian Ridge, an ancient dune line forested by loblolly pine and by a few black cherry trees and old twisty cedars. Once past a long-retired life-saving station, we emerged onto a glaring sand beach. In the surf lay the massive rib cage of a 19th-century schooner, its bones having been buried and resurrected several times as the island's contours shifted.

I began striding down the beach, so as not to waste a second when I could walk at oceanside with nothing, not one thing, man-made as far as I could see: only sand, thicket, water, sky. Then, suddenly, I stopped. In the driftline I spotted some kind of large box, evidently tossed up by a storm. I went closer. It was a television set turned upside down. I had to laugh. The sea had served up a pointed reminder: There was another world out there.

That other world—of possessions, boundaries, and human ambition—has long imposed itself on the island called Cumberland, largest of Georgia's sea islands. About 16 miles long and 3 miles wide at its broadest, Cumberland has always claimed attention. First the Spanish and then the British erected outposts among the spiky palmettos that grow beneath live oaks draped with Spanish moss. Ghosts from those days would still recognize the place: the freshwater ponds patrolled by alligators, the clamorous rookeries in the deep forest, the high bone-white dunes, the unblemished beach where loggerhead turtles come in summer to lay their eggs.

Before the Civil War, slaves cultivated plantation fields of indigo, corn, and cotton. Then, in 1881, a northerner, Thomas Carnegie, brother of steel magnate Andrew Carnegie, bought land on the southern end. After his death his widow purchased most of the island for a family estate.

Vivid traces of the past remain—the outlines of drainage ditches; the chimneys of slave cabins; mansions, some in picturesque ruin, some restored. A few dwellings remain in private hands. Now, however, Cumberland is being allowed to return to wilderness. In 1972 it was designated a national seashore, to be preserved in a "primitive state" and never linked to the mainland by road or causeway. The Park Service intends to acquire all of the island eventually. As part of a program to restore native wildlife, 14 bobcats were set free in the interior in the winter of 1988.

W hat needs absolutely no restoration, no tinkering, is the beach, probably the most magnificent on the North Atlantic coast. It's as dazzling as Rapunzel's hair, stretching for 16 miles, as wide as 200 yards, and rippled with powdery sand. On the day before I arrived by ferry in late January, a northeaster had pounded the shore. Now, under a warm winter sun, I could observe what the sea had given up. Strewn about the flattened beach were thousands of whelk shells; many of these large snails were still alive, trying to bury their turreted shells in the wet sand. I saw cockle shells, sand dollars, purple starfish and orange ones, angel wings, calico crab shells—all hinting at the fantastically rich fauna of the surf zone.

A string of seven brown pelicans skimmed over the waves. Here, near the midpoint of the island, hardly any people were in sight. Most visitors (limited to 300 a day) cluster at the south end where the Park Service ferry from St. Marys drops them. Most of the island is what conservationist David Brower calls "earning territory"—one must earn its pleasures by hiking.

Tramping along, I came upon the stranded carcass of a bottlenose dolphin. A Cumberland resident who had joined me noticed that the belly had been neatly slit open, and said, "Carol must have been here."

Carol Ruckdeschel, the island's unofficial naturalist in residence, performs full necropsies on such casualties for the National Marine Fisheries Service. She has supported herself on government contracts since she was drawn to the place in 1974, leaving a job in Atlanta as a state biologist. "I didn't want to live any more where I couldn't see the stars," she says. I met her at her gray cabin near the north end, and I could smell dolphin innards when I approached the yard. A black vulture with an injured wing peered intently from its cage.

Greeting me from her back porch, Carol looked like an Indian with her sun-darkened face and dark hair worn in two long braids. I mentioned how the dead dolphin had led me to her, and she smiled and pointed to a plastic bucket crammed with the wings and bones of a wild turkey. "I just picked that up," she said. "There are interesting marks on the sternum. Could have been a bobcat kill. As you see, I can't let things go to waste. Why, it'd be a crime. Specimens are biological archives. They help me understand how this island ticks."

Her collection of island specimens now stocks a research museum, inside a large shed in her backyard. "One of the main goals of a wilderness, as I see it, is to enable research to go on," Carol told me as my eye roved over the turtle skulls and snakeskins. "You can't afford to spend years on research and come back and find a subdivision."

Two days later I accepted Carol's invitation—"Let's go tromping"—and joined her on a walk along the edge of the salt marsh. Pushing aside thick vines and prickly bushes with her titanium walking stick, she said she hoped to see an alligator, or at least some gator scat. With an academic colleague, she was trying to prove that alligators had been the island's main predator, and that the ecosystem is unbalanced without a healthy population of them. Her sharp eyes picked out armadillo bones—"The armadillo has only come since the gators have declined"—and the slithery path of a snake. No gator today. "That's all right," she said. "It's beautiful in here. I must get out and walk more! As my mother would say, 'You can't fish without wetting your hook.' "

It was on Cumberland that I began to appreciate the intricacies of the tide-swept marshes that form on the backside of a barrier island. The ocean delivers sand, through tidal inlets or right over the island in storm surges, and coastal rivers pour their nutrient-rich sediments into shallow bays and sounds. Since most marsh plants mature and reproduce within a year, a marsh springs up quickly from a newly formed mud flat.

On a freak 80-degree day in January, I cruised the salt marsh behind Cumberland with Terry Porter, a young, blond-bearded local who has messed around in it since he was a kid. In his 14-foot skiff we slipped up narrow, twisty sloughs, flushing red-winged blackbirds from the tall cordgrass, or *Spartina*. Occasionally a great blue heron would erupt from the olive-drab grass, escaping on long, languid wingbeats. Big-bellied feral horses were out grazing. As the tide ebbed, the dark mud on the banks glistened like a seal's body. From an ill-advised hike in Virginia, I knew I could sink in that goo to my crotch.

With its flatness and its thick even growth, the marsh reminded me of fields in the Midwest. The comparison flatters the farmland. In terms of organic production, a salt marsh can surpass the most fertile wheat or corn field. Its economic value is astounding as well. The 475,000 acres of marsh along the Georgia coast support a seafood industry that contributes 300 million dollars a year to the state economy. *Spartina*, the coarse grass that dominates the wetlands, provides the starting point for the area's prodigious food chain.

At midday Terry pulled the boat up to a low mound of land, one of the Raccoon Keys. The environment changed sharply with a one-foot gain in elevation. Palmetto fronds fanned out above our heads; prickly pear cactus sprouted its red fruits. The ground was chalky white with old oyster and clam shells, left from Indian feasts thousands of years earlier.

From the ancient midden Terry and I could see the crumbling chimneys of Dungeness, the mansion that Thomas Carnegie commissioned. Nearby a high sand dune was invading the marsh. The landscape as much as said that the only thing permanent is change. "You know," remarked Terry, "thinking about what this place will look like makes me see why people want to live forever."

In the southwest of Spain, across the Atlantic from the Virginia barrier islands, visible change accents the life of another wild shore, preserved under the name of Doñana National Park and ranking among Europe's most important nature sanctuaries. On this sandy coast, just northwest of where Europe and Africa lock eyes across the Strait of Gibraltar, 16th-century Spaniards built a line of watchtowers. Lookouts were posted to warn of pirate raids on treasure-laden galleons returning from the New World. Now the stump of one of these towers stands in the surf, the shore having withdrawn from under it, and another is hidden behind a quarter-mile of new dune and forest.

While the coastal contour changes, redrawn by winds and ocean currents, dunes are advancing as well. Inside the 125,000-acre park, windblown sand is burying whole forests of stone pines 25 feet high. Skeletons of dead trees poke up where earlier pinewoods perished. Meanwhile, in some *corrales*, or swales between the mobile sand ridges, new stone pines are braving the air.

Some things don't change at Doñana, however. In October the rains come, flooding once again the delta of the Guadalquivir River. A vast sheet of shallow water slowly spreads across the lowlands, which only weeks before were cracked and withered. Thick reedbeds and watery pastures of sedges and grasses reappear. Then the birds return. Into the reborn *marismas*, or marshes, wild geese, ducks, and wading birds converge from throughout western Europe, to pass the winter in one of the continent's last uncultivated wetlands.

As many as 40,000 greylag geese arrive from Scandinavia. At the time of my visit, in late February, thousands of these large gray migrants still remained, feeding in dense flocks on the fringes of the marsh. At dawn they would etch the sky with their long skeins as they flew to the Cerro de los Ansares, "hill of the geese," a mammoth dune four and a half miles long. There they ingested sand to aid in the digestion of the tough marsh grasses. Ducks were innumerable. Driving on a levee—which park officials jokingly call the River Mountain, so flat is the terrain—I saw marsh waters darkened by great flotillas of teal, wigeon, mallard, pintail, and pochard. In spring these waters and various small islands provide nesting habitat for an abundance of other species. These include stilts, coots, terns, spoonbills, and bitterns as well as some of Europe's scarcest waterfowl, like the ruddy shelduck and the purple gallinule. The long-winged silhouettes of herons were rarely missing from the air. In one afternoon on 100 acres of marsh an ecologist once counted 1,891 birds.

The waters of the marshes are shallow but infested with leeches. That makes a horse man's best friend. One sultry afternoon, I and interpreter Mercedes Lozano accompanied warden Antonio Espinar on a horseback patrol. (Some 35 *guardas* reside in the park, protecting its lonely stretches against poachers.) Slowly the horses splashed across the wetlands, ducks scattering at our approach. Antonio spied an early coot's nest, the nine tan eggs bunched in a reed basket that appeared to float on the water.

Before long Mercedes cried out, *"flamenco!"* and pointed to a thin pink line in the distance. We drew closer. What took shape before us were the long fish-hook necks, the Roman noses, and the pink stilt legs of flamingos, several hundred of them standing in open water. A Mediterranean colony of 15,000 greater flamingos moves to Doñana in late winter to feed in the marshes. At our approach the flamingos began to walk away together, like dandies offended by some vulgar remark. Mercedes clapped her hands and the birds took flight, unveiling the brilliant red of their wings. In the words of a 19th-century bird-watcher in Doñana, they lifted from the marsh "like a flying sunset."

The park takes its name from "Doña Ana"—Lady Anna. Probably this was the reclusive wife of the seventh Duke of Medina Sidonia, admiral-in-chief of the ill-fated Spanish Armada. In 1585 Doña Ana went to live on the ancestral hunting grounds of her husband's family, thus lending her name to the coastal wilderness. Its status as a royal game preserve, where Spanish kings and noblemen hunted red deer and wild boar for six centuries, is what kept Doñana unspoiled. The outside world was finally alerted to its natural wonders when Abel Chapman, an English hunter-naturalist, published accounts of his visits at the turn of the century. It was Chapman who observed its importance to a major flyway between Europe and northern Africa. Seeing the high, shifting dune fields, the open scrubland, and the vast flooded marsh, he wrote that Doñana resembled "a fragment of some savage African solitude."

Conservationists took note when the crowded world came right to Doñana's doorstep. The marshes were being drained for rice fields, the scrub was being turned into eucalyptus plantations, holiday resorts were marching down the beach. In 1964, with the help of the World Wildlife Fund, a biological research preserve was set aside. Five years later a national park was established, and in 1978 it was expanded to its present size, Spain's largest, with another 65,000 acres in protected buffer zones. Coastal wilderness being exceedingly scarce in Europe, officials at Doñana emphasize conservation and research. Camping or unsupervised hiking is prohibited; 200 persons a day may visit the interior on four-hour Land-Rover tours.

*L*ong known to British and Spanish scientists, Doñana is beginning to attract researchers from other lands. "Right now we have people working from Chile, Mexico, Germany, Belgium, and America," said Dr. Miguel Delibes, who directs the biological station. Field scientists bunk at a 16th-century hunting lodge in the park. Laboratories, computers, and other support equipment are available in Seville, 60 miles to the north. "Traditionally most of the studies concerned birds," Dr. Delibes told me, "but now there are more on vegetation, amphibians, and on mammals like the lynx and the mongoose. There is also interest in the marsh hydrography and in the quality and content of the water."

Water pollution worries Dr. Delibes. Pesticides from nearby rice fields have caused several massive bird kills in the past 15 years. Overdevelopment disturbs him too. Recently, however, the government scaled back a large irrigation scheme near the park boundary, and plans for a coastal highway across the park have been shelved. "Intensive agriculture and tourism are not compatible with the park," he said. "The wilderness is not an island, but is affected by everything around it."

Given permission to visit the backcountry if I went with a park official, I usually began each day with a beach ride. I would climb aboard a Land-Rover driven by a ranger, a warden, or a park interpreter and off we would speed down the glorious, unencumbered beach. Broad and flat, it stretches 12 miles between the resort town of Matalascañas and the mouth of the Guadalquivir.

Rousing gulls and oystercatchers as we went, we would often see local fisher-men dragging in the surf for coquinas, delicious small clams. Oyster shells with purple splotches and cuttlebones—the interior shell of the cuttlefish—crunched under our wheels. Several times I sighted a peregrine on the top of one of the old watchtowers.

At some point we would turn and cut across the stark dune fields, which are six miles wide in places, and drop into one of the corrales. There the pine-woods offered relief from wind and sun. During the migration seasons the parasol-like stone pines are full of warblers, flycatchers, and orioles. One day I spotted—with binoculars—a hovering Spanish imperial eagle, identifiable by the white band across the front of its wings. "There are only 200 of those birds in the world!" my guide exclaimed. Doñana shelters 32 of them.

Reaching the marshes, we would conduct a flamingo check—we saw them every day—and then watch terns nosedive into the water or gray herons spear fish with sudden stabs of neck and beak. Often a small herd of fallow deer, conspicuous with their broad, mooselike racks, would splash across a flooded meadow at our arrival.

The scrubland in the northern reaches of the park offered the most varied sightings. A rare Spanish lynx, sitting on its haunches on the bank of a slough, allowed us a peek at its tufted ears and spotted coat before it sauntered into the bulrushes. Kites lived up to their names, large forktailed birds swooping and twirling on thermal air currents. About a dozen baleful vultures perched on one dead cork oak—among them the imposing black vulture, the light brown griffon, and the striking black-and-white Egyptian vulture. We even came upon a one-humped camel, a leftover from the filming of *Lawrence of Arabia* 20 years earlier.

The array of wildlife at Doñana was impressive. But I could never fool myself into thinking I was in some vast nowhere. After all, this was Europe. Late one morning, I was staring intently at a dignified pair of white storks standing on a nest in the top of a cork oak. I rested my eyes by scanning the open, parklike expanse. And there in the near distance rose a church spire from the pilgrim-age village of El Rocío. I remembered the prophecy of the peaceable kingdom, where prey and predator and playful child are safe together. Maybe in such a setting wilderness would be safe forever.

But then again, perhaps someday a developed coast, and not a wild one, will become the exception. If, in the next century, ocean levels continue to rise dra-matically, whole stretches of crowded coastline may become uninhabited again. It was strange—unnerving—to stand on wild beaches in Europe and in America and realize that untamed shores not only symbolize the past but may also represent the future. With the thunder of the surf in my ears, the force of wind in my face, and the rasp of the sand at my feet, I was not one to doubt the power of change.

FOLLOWING PAGES: High tide laves autumn-gold Spartina *grass at a salt marsh behind barrier islands of the Virginia Coast Reserve.*

JOHN M. HALL

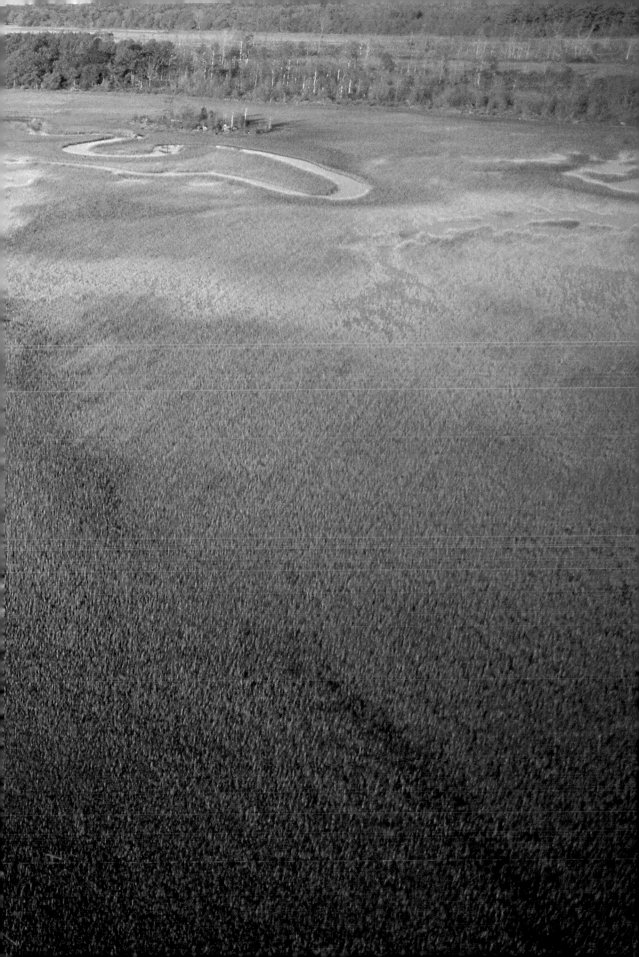

Royal terns with fish in their beaks drop in to feed their young at a nesting colony on Fishermans Island in the

DAVID ALAN HARVEY (BOTH); FRED WHITEHEAD (FOLLOWING PAGES)

Virginia group. A hollow in the sand serves as a nest for black skimmer hatchlings on Metomkin Island.

FOLLOWING PAGES: After a January northeaster, cockle and whelk shells brighten Cumberland Island's beach.

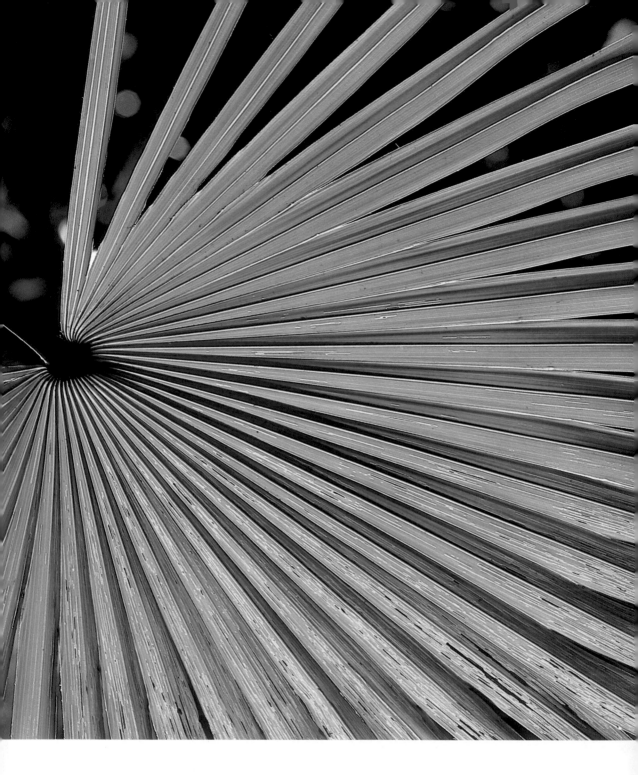

On Cumberland Island sharp-edged
saw palmetto shades small reptiles like
the molting green anole at right.
Baby alligators share the freshwater
ponds with adults as long as ten feet.

FOLLOWING PAGES: Live oaks dripping
Spanish moss reclaim cutover fields on
Cumberland; wild turkeys, snakes,
bobcats, and feral hogs rustle about in
the scratchy palmetto understory.

FRED WHITEHEAD (ALL); © DAVID MUENCH 1988 (FOLLOWING PAGES)

Wind-rippled sand, advancing as fast as nine feet a year, invades a young forest of stone pines on the restless coast of Spain's Doñana National Park. Dune fields, scrub, and marshes supply habitat for 60-odd resident bird species and some 170 migrants, as well as reptiles and rare mammals. Kings and grandees of Spain hunted here for centuries. Below, the Guadalquivir River, half a mile wide at its mouth, separates the park from the wine-producing town Sanlúcar de Barrameda.

FOLLOWING PAGES: Greater flamingos cross the moonlit waters of Lucio del Membrillo; as many as 15,000 winter here, feeding in the brackish shallows.

DENNIS CHAMBERLIN (BOTH); JUAN A. FERNÁNDEZ / INCAFO (FOLLOWING PAGES)

WARM TEMPERATE COASTS:

A Portfolio

Beyond the 25th parallels north and south, the notion of seasons changes. The tropical regime of wet and dry gives way to the more complicated shadings of warm and cool. Summer and winter become realities. On the coastlines of the warm temperate zone—roughly, between the 25th and 40th parallels—mild winters and warm-to-hot summers define seasonal rhythms. With the exception of occasional cold snaps, the winters are so mild that alligators bask in January sun on Georgia's Cumberland Island, while rosemary and lavender perfume the air of Spain's Coto Doñana. To escape the months of ice, great flocks of northern birds—snow geese and Canada geese in America, greylag and bean geese in Europe—migrate south to such shores.

Summers are usually oppressive in the humid areas on the southeastern flanks of six continents. Here precipitation is spread throughout the year. In the zone's other great subtype, the Mediterranean, summers bring low humidity, scant rain, and—usually—clear skies. Aside from the Mediterranean littorals that gave this subtype its name, this much-desired climate is found on southwest coasts of Australia and South Africa. It also appears in California, where summer fogs often form over chilly offshore waters.

Positioned between the equatorial and the polar extremes, these shores are vulnerable to storms from both directions. Hurricanes—or typhoons, or cyclones—strike from the tropics. From the poles, winter storm fronts hurl gale winds and damaging waves, or plunge temperatures below freezing.

Such storms keep undeveloped coastlines in natural flux. Waves pound away at cliffs, sand dunes bury marsh and forest, barrier islands retreat shoreward. These temperate shores have attracted humankind for many centuries, but today's high-price development may become a high-risk endeavor.

Strong with spring rain, an oceanbound creek flashes past wild callas on a lonely stretch of California's Big Sur Coast.

© DAVID MUENCH 1988

*S*alt-tolerant sea figs stabilize loose sand at Point Reyes National Seashore. On the horizon

JAMES H. KATZ

a summer fog bank forms over the cold offshore waters of central California.

*S*ea foam streaks deserted Wildcat
Beach after a winter storm at craggy
Point Reyes. Heavy Pacific Ocean
breakers and strong undertow have

DEWITT JONES (BOTH)

ground and chipped a lustrous abalone
shell tossed up on a pebble beach.

oaring in threat—or battle—stance, two male northern elephant seals display defiant rivalry at a winter rookery on Año Nuevo Island. More than 3,000 congregate in this stark reserve 55 miles south of San Francisco. The two-ton bulls, some of them 16 feet long, arrive first and fight for dominance—sometimes to the death. Smaller by several feet and about a ton, the females follow; many will give birth to a pup, then mate for the next year. In spring all return to open sea. Hunted for oil-rich blubber, the species neared extinction by 1890; one remote, inaccessible Mexican beach sheltered a herd of fewer than 100. From these descend about 100,000 animals, rescued and protected by Mexico and the U.S.

© FRANS LANTING

In sandy shallows at Izu Oceanic Park, Japan, a giant spider crab—a small female—represents

© DAVID DOUBILET

the world's largest crustacean. The record claw-span for the species: 12 feet.

DESERT COASTS:

Harsh Littorals

By Loren McIntyre

t was too quiet, he told me long afterward. I've spent much of my life in South America, and made a great many friends there, and picked up a lot of stories along the wild reaches of its western coast. Julio Galán's is one of the most dramatic.

That uncanny stillness snapped Don Julio out of an afternoon nap in the small cabin of his barge moored to a buoy off Pimentel, a seaport in northern Peru. The barge seemed motionless, no longer rolling with the ceaseless ocean swells that come into the roadstead from the South Pacific. For an instant he thought it had drifted onto the beach. But no; there was no sound of surf. He jerked open the cabin door. The sun, as always at this hour, was a pale orange disk sinking into sea-born fog.

"The tide had ebbed so far that it left my barge sitting on the bottom. All around me fish were flopping on the sand. Some boys came running to pick them up. I screamed, 'No, no, no!' But too late. A distant hissing sound began to grow so loud it seemed as if all the steam locomotives that haul sugar to the pier were arriving at once. But the pier was empty—and the water was gone."

Out of the fog roared a wave that blocked the sun. Julio Galán recalls only instant nightfall and noise. Seawater crushed him, choked him, blinded him, and completely confused him. All he can say for sure, nowadays, is that his barge was lifted into the streets, the receding flow washed him back into the harbor, and at daybreak friends spotted him clinging to a buoy.

Don Julio had survived a tsunami, one of a series of seismic sea waves that devastated Pimentel on November 20, 1960. As in ancient times, the disaster inspired a religious procession. Each year, worshipers in Pimentel parade a

Huge mystery relief—"El Candelabro"
—faces seaward from a desert slope on
Peru's Paracas Peninsula, a wildlife preserve.

LOREN McINTYRE

huge cross along the beach. After the ceremony, young fishermen compete for the *caballito de totora* championship, riding the waves to shore on "little horses." These are one-man reed fishing craft like those depicted on 1,500-year-old ceramics found in desert tombs. Many a north coast fisherman still paddles his pony out to sea at daybreak. He lowers a baited hook onto rocks that he can detect by immersing a paddle vertically and pressing an ear to it— or, in deep water, his teeth. A sandy or muddy bottom yields no sign, but when a fisherman senses a vibration and "the rock begins to cry—*ya llora la peña*," he drops his stone anchor. Caballitos return at midday, before the afternoon winds stir up whitecaps; none were caught by the sundown tsunami of 1960.

Such waves are generated by such events as major volcanic eruptions or undersea earthquakes. They can strike the South American coast from as far away as Asia or Alaska. Although they're detected in the Pacific about five hundred times a century, only one in five plays havoc. In deep water they travel several hundred miles an hour, and are only a few inches or a few feet high. When the sea floor slopes upward, they go slower and begin to peak. A wave nearing the shore—a *tsu-nami*, Japanese for "great harbor wave"—may reach spectacular heights, with catastrophic results. Following an earthquake in 1746, a 60-foot wave killed 5,000 to 7,000 people in Lima's seaport, Callao.

The mantle of mist that hid the approaching tsunami from Julio Galán forms over the north-flowing Peru Current, also called the Humboldt Current after the scientist who found it unusually cold for the torrid zone. The current cools the tropical air just above it, causing fog and a low cloud bank to form along the coastline for much of the year, while higher levels of air remain warm. This temperature inversion has inhibited rainfall along South America's west coast, from latitude 30° south to 4° S, for much of the past ten or fifteen million years, helping to make the region one of the driest deserts on earth.

While that narrow edge of the continent is largely barren, the adjacent ocean teems with marine life, from diatoms to whales. The Peru Current flows as far north as the Equator, yet its dense biomass consists mainly of subantarctic species. A single quart of its water may hold 40,000 of the tiny plants and animals called plankton, from the Greek word for "drifting." I couldn't see ten feet through that organic soup when diving into a rusty shipwreck off Callao to spear a few fish for a picnic on the beach. That was shortly after World War II, and I was using an escape vest from a German submarine. Inside the hull, a huge shape materialized out of the gloom. Fright made me hyperventilate on pure oxygen and I wondered if I were hallucinating. But the spooky shape turned out to be a *lobo de mar*, the mammal called sea wolf in Spanish and sea lion in English. This one wasn't belligerent, just curious.

Upwelling from deep ocean layers along the continental wall brings nutrients to the surface, where solar energy activates the rich biomass. The water is coldest closest to the shore. When Alexander von Humboldt first sighted the Pacific Ocean, he rushed into the surf with thermometer in hand. Later, on a voyage from Callao to Ecuador during Christmas week of 1802, he took the seawater temperature every day. His low readings show no trace of El Niño. Named for the Christ Child, this is a warm countercurrent that sometimes steals down the coast from the tropics around Yuletide, upsetting marine ecology. The term has been expanded to encompass episodic heating of the equatorial Pacific and its effects on global climate; the catastrophic El Niño of 1982-83 cost the world 8.65 billion dollars in estimated losses.

Of all forms of life along this coast, seabirds are the most conspicuous. It's easiest to see the value of the cormorants, pelicans, and gannets or boobies, classified as "guano birds" because their droppings are harvested and sold as commercial fertilizer. Recently, to visit seabird rookeries, I boarded a launch that carried fresh water and provisions from Pimentel to Lobos de Tierra, the northernmost of 40-odd desert islands strung along the Peruvian coast.

W e cruised a liquid mirror warped by ceaseless swells born of gales far to the southwest. Now and then the mirror was splintered by agitat ed schools of small fish and by boobies; after cruising at about 100 feet, they would wheel in formation and dive like kamikaze aircraft into the froth. Porpoises escorted us all day. After dark the water was full of phosphorescence outlining ghostly shapes that I thought at first were sharks. When one surfaced I realized they were sea lions. The naturalist Robert Cushman Murphy gave an enchanting description in his 1925 classic, *Bird Islands of Peru:* ". . . a lobo burst forth, as if from a molten firmament, and then plunged again in pursuit of the fiery comets whose heads were fleeing fishes."

Although Lobos de Tierra is governed by a resident agent of the guano bureau, birds really own it. *Piqueros* (Peruvian boobies, *Sula variegata*) occupy acres of flatlands, about three nests to a square yard; at other guano islands they nest on ledges in fearsome cliffs. Each produces as much as five ounces of guano a day. *Camanayes* (blue-footed boobies, *Sula nebouxii*) nest where they please, neither budging from a pathway nor heeding a visitor who knelt close by to photograph their goose-stepping courtships. High ground at the edge of sea cliffs is crowded with families of big pelicans (*Pelecanus occidentalis thagus*) peculiar to the Peru Current. Their young, which gain several pounds before they grow feathers, strongly suggest prehistoric reptiles.

Rocky islets just offshore hold harems of sea lion cows and their pups, guarded by bulls whose necks, thick as a bison's, are scarred by sharp rocks and the tusks of rivals. These seraglios stink to high heaven. As at nearby islands, the surf is too rough, the rocks too jagged, and the water too cold for thin-skinned human swimmers.

Once called "the most valuable birds in the world," *guanayes* nest on islands south of Lobos de Tierra and on headlands protected by high walls. These cormorants, *Phalacrocorax bougainvilleii,* became Peru's best money-makers when their excrement began to be sold overseas 150 years ago. Black-jacketed, white-breasted, they would fly for miles in incredibly long columns, alight to form enormous rafts bending to the swells, and duck-dive into the cold sea to gulp anchovies. One adult's crop can hold as many as six dozen of these four-to five-inch fish. At nightfall the birds would return to their nests and regurgitate their catch to feed their offspring. As they defecated around their feather-lined nests, a mineral-rich rim of ordure built up and hardened.

Lacking rain to wash them away, some guano deposits thickened over the years to 150 feet and more. An estimated twenty million tons had encrusted offshore islands by the 1840s, when farmers abroad learned what Peruvians had known for many centuries: that it was excellent fertilizer. Rich in nitrogen, potassium, and phosphorus, it's far more effective than barnyard manure.

When commercial exploitation began, hundreds of foreign sailing ships anchored around the islands, waiting as long as three months to load gunnysacks reeking of ammonia. Chinese coolies, hired as contract labor to mine the deposits, were so brutally treated that many committed suicide by leaping from the cliffs; their corpses became mummified in guano. By 1869, loading was improved by long canvas chutes. In U.S. terms, guano costing $10 a ton at the coast might sell in London for $100 (it costs $450 a ton in Peru today).

By the end of the century the deposits were almost gone. Peru took action to limit the harvest and protect the birds. By 1950 more than 90 million guano birds crowded the islands, according to Robert Cushman Murphy, with ten trillion anchovies as their food supply. But, Dr. Murphy warned, anchovies were "vanishing into a vast new maw, factories that grind them into fish meal for cattle and poultry food."

Money talked louder than his warning. By 1970 more than a hundred fish meal factories were smelling up desert shores and seaports—and starving the guano birds. The anchovy catch of 14 million tons amounted to one-sixth of all fish caught everywhere, in fresh water and salt. Peru led the world's fisheries nations in tonnage, but overfishing had wrecked the ecosystem. It broke a link in the basic food chain: nutrients to plankton to anchovies to guano birds. Most of the anchovies ended up in the stomachs of livestock elsewhere.

Starvation and disease decimated the great seabird populations. Guanayes collapsed in flight; waves piled their carcasses hip deep on the desert shores. In 1972 El Niño's warm water added to the debacle. In 1973 the catch fell to two million tons; now Peru stood sixth on the world fisheries list. The damage spread. To meet demands for livestock feed, farmers switched to soybeans. That caused a rice shortage in Brazil, which caused pioneers to plant rice in the ashes of rain forests. Food for many lands had depended on the bounty of the cold current off the wild shores of South America.

Strict control has repaired some of the damage. In 1988 Peru netted five million tons (most of the fish meal went to China). The bird population holds at 4 percent of the 1950 peak, but guanayes no longer fly by in unbroken columns so long they take five hours to pass a headland or a topmast. I haven't seen a column take as long as a minute for many years. Some guano is still being scraped off the rookeries—but primarily for local use.

El Niño, incidentally, doesn't flow far enough south to affect the schools of sardines along the Chilean coast, and there are fewer seabirds there, but fishermen follow the fish day and night, some aided by spotter aircraft.

Packet boats were the sensible means of travel up and down the desert coast early in this century, but now the choice is between air and land. It's no great feat to drive the desert in one week, from the lush green fields of Ecuador to the pine forests of southern Chile. The Pan American Highway threads the entire 2,500 miles of beige and brown countryside squeezed between the cold sea and the cold heights of the Andes, the rain barrier that helps to form the desert.

Prevailing winds from the Amazon Basin force wet air against the eastern slopes of the Andes. It rises, cools, and condenses into clouds that fail to cross the continental divide. They dump about ten feet of rain a year into the dense forests of the eastern slopes, and some snow on the summits. Only during January and February, the wettest months in the Peruvian highlands, does enough water spill west of the summits to send scores of short rivers cascading down mountainsides and across the desert to the sea. Rains cease in April. By September all but a dozen rivers will have run dry before they reach the Pacific, yielding the last of their water to irrigate farms and to sustain towns.

Many of the coastal settlements were founded by Indians, as early as 2500 B.C. At first these aborigines lived on shellfish and plants gathered along the shores. Later they created oases by irrigating patches of fertile soil, and their harvests of corn and beans supported the rise of city-states.

Driving the *Panamericana* today, you can expect a riverine oasis every eight to eighty miles. You slow down for children and pushcart vendors, or stop at a fruit stand. Some oases are wide; the city of Lima has spread for miles beyond the dusty border of the oasis that I knew when I went to live there in 1947. It is now ten times as populous, holding eight million people—a majority of the inhabitants of the west coast desert.

One *limeño* I sorely miss is the late Georg Petersen, a leading geologist who understood the desert better than anyone I know. In my old friend's library I used to pore over maps while planning my own field trips. Petersen led me to think of desert expeditions as traveling back in time. As he explained, "This is a very old desert. Since it has rarely rained in ten or fifteen million years you can see ancient tectonic and volcanic features—as exposed as a Martian landscape. On the other side of the Andes such formations are invisible, covered by forest. Between Ilo and Tacna in southern Peru you can cross empty sands still rutted by wagon tracks and the marching feet of long-vanished armies. In a wetter climate such vestiges would have been erased by weathering or disguised by vegetation."

This aridity has preserved another record of the past, on view in Lima's museums: a prehistoric chronicle as told by many thousands of artifacts unearthed from tombs beneath the sand. Some of the story is marvelous and much is murderous. An ancient embroidery, for example, its colors still brilliant, depicts warriors' delight in taking human heads as trophies.

Southbound from Tacna, you cross a waste of sand dunes to enter Chile. There the coastal desert acquires a proper name, Atacama, from its former Indian inhabitants. No one speaks their language any more, but the desert is so dry that their forlorn graveyards reveal almost as much about the occupants' culture as do Egyptian tombs. Thousands of mummies have been recovered, their flesh parched by natural means, their skulls deformed to sugarloaf shapes by binding in infancy.

No desert could be much drier. Northern seaports in Chile go for years without recording precipitation of even one-tenth of a millimeter, the thickness of a sheet of newspaper. The Pan American Highway veers inland; a coastal escarpment rises sharply from the sea, as high as 3,000 feet. The cliff keeps beach sand from blowing inland and the Atacama surface is crusty, much of it fairly flat. The highway is often fenced by power poles, scale markers on a giant's yardstick. Drooping wires converge with the pavement at infinity, as if sketched by Dali. The light seldom shimmers in this chilly air.

Inca armies marched down from the Peruvian highlands and conquered the *atacameños* in the 1470s, about the time Francisco Pizarro was born in Spain. After Pizarro overthrew the Inca empire, his countryman Diego de Almagro led 570 Spaniards and 12,000 Indians into the Atacama in search of gold. These "Men of Chile" found only disenchantment and death. Survivors returned to Peru so embittered they eventually murdered Pizarro.

About the time of independence from Spain, in 1821, few traveled the Atacama except *cateadores,* prospectors looking for gold and silver and for ancient graves that might hold both. Many a prospector stayed up all night, hoping that daybreak would let him follow the *alicante,* a legendary bird whose wings glowed gold or silver depending upon which metal it ate. If the alicante felt menaced before reaching its feeding place, it would fold its wings and disappear. Then the disappointed prospector might become just another *empampado,* a desert rat, lost and hungry and thirsty, sunburned in the daytime and shivering all the Atacama night.

The Atacama still belonged to Peru and Bolivia when cateadores discovered vast deposits of a substance they called *salitre*—saltpeter; that's potassium nitrate, used since the 12th century for making gunpowder. In fact their new find was sodium nitrate, but it also proved useful as an ingredient of explosives and, later on, as fertilizer. Like guano, salitre is soluble in water; rain would have washed it away. Unlike guano, its origin is a mystery. There are many conflicting theories as to why it occurs in this region and nowhere else on earth, but most of them agree that millions of years of rainlessness had a lot to do with forming layers thick enough to have commercial value.

The wild shores of the Atacama began to bustle in the 1830s with shipments of nitrates to England and the United States. Salitre may have helped propel bullets in the Crimean War and explode shells at Gettysburg. It certainly brought ruin to Peru and riches to Chile in the War of the Pacific—sometimes called the "Salitre War" because it began when Chile seized the nitrate mines. The carnage was ghastly. As a naval adviser to Peru many years ago, I realized that if blood could make a garden grow, the seaside sands of Chile and Peru would have burst into bloom.

Both countries had equipped their navies with ironclad warships built in England. In 1879 the vessels battled for most of the year, up and down the desert shores. At Iquique, an Atacama port, Peru's *Huáscar* rammed the ship of a young Chilean officer, Arturo Prat. Prat drew his sword, boarded the enemy ship, and perished. Today, Arturo Prat is Chile's greatest naval hero.

Eventually the Chileans captured the *Huáscar* near an uninhabited peninsula. The day of the battle, October 8, is a solemn national holiday in both Chile and Peru. The fallen Peruvian admiral, Miguel Grau, was immortalized. I have seen so many likenesses of Grau—photographs, portraits, busts, statues—that I could recognize him instantly on the street. So could any Peruvian older than six. The 1879-83 war is still being fought in wardrooms and at Peru's Naval

War College. Both Chile and Peru maintain fleets ready to pick up where Prat and Grau left off—if provoked.

Grau's defeat left vulnerable 1,800 miles of Peruvian seacoast, defenseless against amphibious landings. By 1883 Chilean armies had prevailed. They went home in 1884, taking all sorts of booty. Thus Peru lost the Atacama and its nitrate mines, and Bolivia lost access to the sea.

For half a century, nitrate earnings brought wealth into Chile. Then synthetic fertilizers captured the market. During the Great Depression of the 1930s most of the Atacama nitrate works shut down. The desert mineral that cost thousands of lives—that led to the chiseling of thousands of names on memorial obelisks in Chile, Peru, and Bolivia—is hardly worth a fistfight today. The bleak Atacama is haunted by ghost towns that Chileans call *cementerios*, cemeteries as woebegone as the pillaged tombs of the early Americans.

Even so, the alicante's wings still glow at daybreak—with a reddish luster. A few years ago prospectors took an interest in a shapeless hill in the Atacama wasteland, a mound called La Escondida, "the hidden place." In 1984 I saw them drilling dozens of exploratory holes. In 1989 I accompanied aides of international investors to La Escondida. They said they were investing a billion dollars in the site: "We expect it to become the world's richest copper mine."

Some of my most vivid memories of the desert coast involve Paracas Bay, about 150 miles south of Lima. I first saw it in 1948, aboard the Peruvian cruiser *Almirante Grau*. My wife, Sue, drove down for the weekend, and we went out sailing. The stiff afternoon winds dismasted our boat and began sweeping us seaward. I waved an undershirt and made jokes about riding the Peru Current 4,000 miles to Polynesia, as Thor Heyerdahl had just done on his raft *Kon-Tiki*. Luckily an officer on the *Grau* sighted my distress signal in time.

In 1955 I returned to film *Mar de Sangre (Sea of Blood)*, a documentary for a whaling company, and put to sea one night on a rusty whale-chaser manned largely by Norwegians. At daybreak the lookout in the crow's nest shouted *"Cachalotes!"* Literally "sperm whales," it's the Peruvian equivalent of "Thar she blows and sparm at that!" We were steaming through a pod of whales: at least one bull and a dozen cows. The captain called for full speed, 12 knots. A sperm whale can swim that fast, but not for long. The bull sounded, but another surfaced and the captain chased him. "Maybe he's out of oxygen. Won't dive. He's maybe 60 feet . . . 60 tons . . . 60 years old."

Almost on the surface, the whale parted the waves like a nuclear submarine. His enormous gray head was streaked with 20-foot rows of white disks. "Sucker-cup scars from squid tentacles. The whale's outer skin sloughs off when it fights and feeds on giant squid a thousand feet down in the dark," the captain said. "Go, gringo. Watch from the crow's nest."

I climbed the mast as the captain ran to the foredeck to aim and fire his harpoon gun. I saw the harpoon line follow the projectile into the whale, saw his flukes arch higher than the bow of the boat as he made one last desperate dive, saw the line whirling into the cold blue ocean, flashing a colored stripe at 100 meters, 200 meters, 300 meters. . . . When the rope finally slackened, I watched a sailor take it to a winch and haul the whale to the surface with a clattering of gears. After the kill, both boat and victim floated in a widening pond of blood, and I climbed down from the crow's nest feeling more bereaved than ever I had during World War II.

The last time I visited Paracas, in April 1989, the whaling station was shut down. The old motel had grown into the four-star Hotel Paracas, but the desert shore was uncluttered by developers. Here, in 1975, inspired by Peruvian conservationist Felipe Benavides, the government had created South America's first marine wildlife reserve. It includes the Paracas Peninsula and the Ballestas Islands, ten miles out in the Pacific. The hotel manager offered the safest way to visit the Ballestas: "Our boats have twin 175-horsepower outboards and skilled pilots to keep you off the rocks. Go with Julián. He's the best."

April 6 was a day to remember. We sped out to sea, the boat slamming from wave to wave. Stony spires materialized out of early fog. Enormous swells surged up the Ballestas cliffs and rebounded. The backwash peaked against incoming waves; the boat teetered on steep crests. Never in years at sea have I known choppier water. The islands seemed to have no lee side, no place to land. "Anyway it's forbidden," said Julián.

The Ballestas seem to be summits of an emerging island that is being lashed by the sea and hammered to pieces almost as fast as it rises above the surface. Waves explode against cliffs, gouging grottoes, carving caves, and finally piercing clean through the rock to form archways open at both ends, supporting tableland on top. It would be splendid to cruise through the great galleries when the sea is calm—as it is once or twice a year, according to Julián.

He kept the stern of the boat aimed seaward so its propellers could grab green water if a wave started to break under us. We had splendid views of the wildlife protected here. Sea lions in the thousands sunned on the rocks or thronged into the white water to study us. Flights of Inca terns wheeled in and out of dark caves. Boobies preened on unlikely crags, and pelicans strutted in profile along the headlands, so that from some angles the Ballestas resembled bombed-out castles with small dinosaurs patrolling their battlements.

April 7 was a day to forget, although it started well. I planned a drive on the Paracas Peninsula, a 60-square-mile slab of utter desert that thrusts into the ocean south of the Ballestas. On surrounding shores its permanent residents live beneath high cliffs: mobs of sea lions, crowds of sea birds, and millions of small crustaceans (*mui muis*) in the surf. A few humans live along the beaches of the bay. There's also a transient population: about 50 species of North American migratory birds, tourists from all the continents of the Northern Hemisphere, and even occasional highwaymen.

Never before, in a lifetime of travel in South America, have I needed a bodyguard, but the hotel manager thought it risky for me to go alone. So I took along an off-duty policeman from the town of Pisco, a young man I called Willy. He came in civilian clothes, with a knowing smile and a concealed snub-barreled revolver. At first he told me about his years of service in the highlands, fighting terrorists. As we got better acquainted he showed me pictures of his wife and his children, ages one and three.

We drove slowly along the edge of great seacliffs and parked above the Mirador de Lobos ("sea lion lookout") at the end of the peninsula. I could hear sea lions roaring and breakers thundering on rocks 200 feet below. I walked to the brink and looked down. Shots rang out—I whirled. *"Por Dios!"* breathed Willy. Three masked men were running downhill toward us, firing pistols.

Willy knelt and emptied his gun at them, dropping one man. A bullet ripped my pants and a sock, knocking me off my feet but barely nicking my ankle.

I lay prone. The fusillade stopped. A gunman kicked and pistol-whipped me, bloodying my head. At gunpoint he forced me uphill to unlock the car. Once I glanced back. At the lookout, one masked man was lifting another to his feet. Where was Willy? Wounded? Dead? Thrown over the cliff?

As I opened the car door, my assailant fired at me. *Click.* He fired again. *Click.* He shifted the empty gun to his left hand to fish for bullets in his right pants pocket. I grabbed at the gun. We struggled. He pulled away. I hurled the car keys downhill and sprinted uphill—not easy in sand—hoping a bullet in the back wouldn't smash my spine.

But the highwayman went after the keys, then helped carry his bleeding partner to the car. To my surprise they all drove away. Fearing Willy? Hurrying to a doctor? They didn't know that the trunk was full of photo and electronic equipment—yet.

Fearing they would return to finish me off, I hurried down to search along the precipice, shouting "Willy! Willy!" Only the surf replied.

Dry mouthed, feeling very vulnerable, I jogged six miles to a fishing village and hitched a ride into Pisco to organize a search party. Hours later I returned with four policemen, an Air Force doctor, and two Navy men skilled at rappelling. They roped their way down the cliff to the sea lion rookery and soon came back up, shaking their heads: "No one could survive that surf."

We drove back to police headquarters in silence. What a day off for Willy! What could I do for his wife, his children?

A sentry at the police station was holding a Kalashnikov assault rifle. Too bad Willy hadn't had one. . . . The sentry grinned at me: "Señor, we have a surprise inside." There on a bunk, nursing a lacerated foot, sat Willy. He had managed to hide on a ledge sheltered by the rim of the cliff, and had not dared to answer when he heard me call. "I thought they might be holding a gun at your head," he explained. He had waited two hours to be sure the coast was clear, climbed back to the rim, and walked out to safety—painfully, having lost a shoe in the fracas. And next day we learned that the thieves had dumped their dead accomplice in a cotton field near the *Panamericana.* They abandoned the car in a pre-Inca ruin, but stole my cameras.

The theft put an end to my filming for the trip. That was about as traumatic as being shot at, but I reflected that my misadventure was a small event in local history, a very small event in the cosmic scheme of things along one of the world's wilder shores. Someday I shall finish the circuit of the Paracas Peninsula—and cruise into the dark grottoes of the Ballestas Islands when the seas are less chaotic.

FOLLOWING PAGES: Endemic to Peruvian shores, Inca terns feast with sea lions in the cold Peru Current at the Ballestas Islands.

LOREN McINTYRE

"Little horses" of the sea, reed boats known as caballitos *resemble surfboards upended to dry as daylight sinks into sea-born fog. Come dawn, traditional ocean fishermen in northern Peru will paddle the tiny craft seaward across bucking surf. A mounted caballito captain (opposite) works with customary line and hook; a net abaft holds his catch. His ancestors fished from similar one-man boats, according to images found on pre-Columbian pottery.*

LOREN McINTYRE (BOTH)

Pocket bays lined with boulders notch Peru's dry coast. Wedging of the Nazca Plate under the continent has uplifted the shoreline, and continues to inch it higher. Working the Peru Current (below), a crew pulls in a gill net. Catches of anchovy have yet to recover fully from El Niño, a warm coastal countercurrent that decimated Peru's fish populations in 1972.

LOREN McINTYRE (BOTH AND FOLLOWING PAGES)

FOLLOWING PAGES: *Highly valued as organic fertilizer, guano supplied by Peruvian cormorants whitens a rookery.*

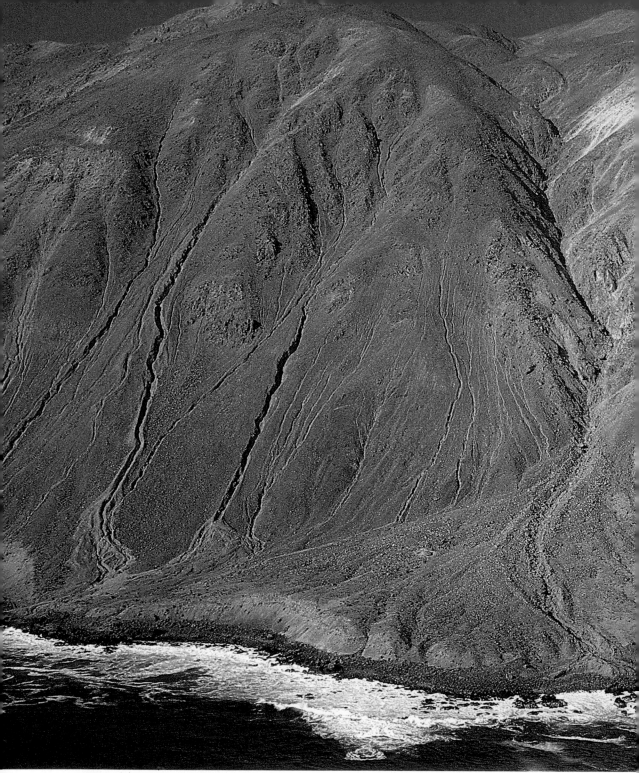

LOREN McINTYRE (ABOVE AND FOLLOWING PAGES)

*In wrinkled cliffs, the Atacama—
the world's driest desert—meets
the sea. Inland from Chile's coast,*

extreme aridity has preserved
such valuable minerals as sodium
nitrate, once used in explosives.

FOLLOWING PAGES: *La Portada, a*
wave-cut arch, serves as landmark
for the mineral port of Antofagasta.

DESERT SHORES:

A Portfolio

Twins deceptively linked, coastal desert and sea are inseparable extremes. Together they embody a realm of blinding sunshine and dazzling paradox. How can land be desert-dry where it meets a rolling ocean or a spacious gulf?

Cold ocean currents offer one answer. When warm coastal air brushes chilly waters, a temperature inversion—a layer of cold moist air trapped under a layer of warm air—can occur. Fog forms instead of rain clouds. Winds blowing parallel to the coast pin the ribbons of sea mist close to shore. Then, denied as much as ten inches of rainfall a year, the ocean's borderland qualifies as desert. Thus the Peru Current, flowing north from Antarctica, influences South America's hyperarid Atacama and Peruvian Deserts. The cold Benguela Current keeps Africa's Namib so thirsty that its shore became infamous as the Skeleton Coast. Here the winds build dunes as high as 800 feet: the planet's highest.

Mountains rule Baja's Central Desert, baking in a rain shadow on the Gulf of California. Peaks of the peninsula's mountain spine steal rain from clouds billowing with Pacific moisture, leaving dry wind to parch the lowland. Surreal vegetation flourishes here, including 80 endemic species of cacti.

Barren winds gusting across North Africa or the Arabian Peninsula chafe the alkaline shores of one of the world's most extraordinary bodies of water. Aridity hostile to many land animals blesses life in the Red Sea. Free of cloudy river sediments, its warm crystalline waters nurture lavish coral terraces, rare reef fishes, and scores of other sea creatures found nowhere else.

The earth's desert shores extend for thousands of miles, in North and South America, Africa, southwest Asia, and Australia. Without exception they cleave a realm where opposing extremes engage in one of nature's most fascinating dramas of duality—dryness and dampness, sand and sea.

A cresting dune—one of the world's highest— bares an oryx skull in Africa's Namib Desert, a sand sea amazingly rich in animal life.

© JIM BRANDENBURG

109

og hangs between the Namib's "great dune sea" and islands flecked with flamingos. It forms

© JIM BRANDENBURG

as warm South Atlantic trade winds blow across the cold, north-flowing Benguela Current.

*S*unset leap of a spinner dolphin breaks the calm in the Strait of Tiran east of Egypt. Hazy in

© DAVID DOUBILET

the heat, distant mountains on the Sinai Peninsula tumble toward the Red Sea.

*R*ed Sea fantasia: Batfish cluster for safety, while the eye of a humphead wrasse roves for prey. Swift evaporation and low rainfall

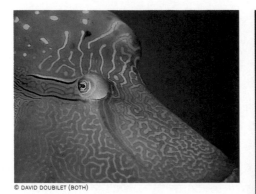

© DAVID DOUBILET (BOTH)

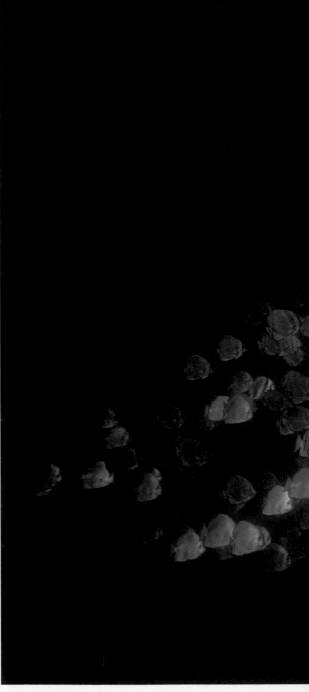

leave Red Sea waters saltier
than any of the open oceans.

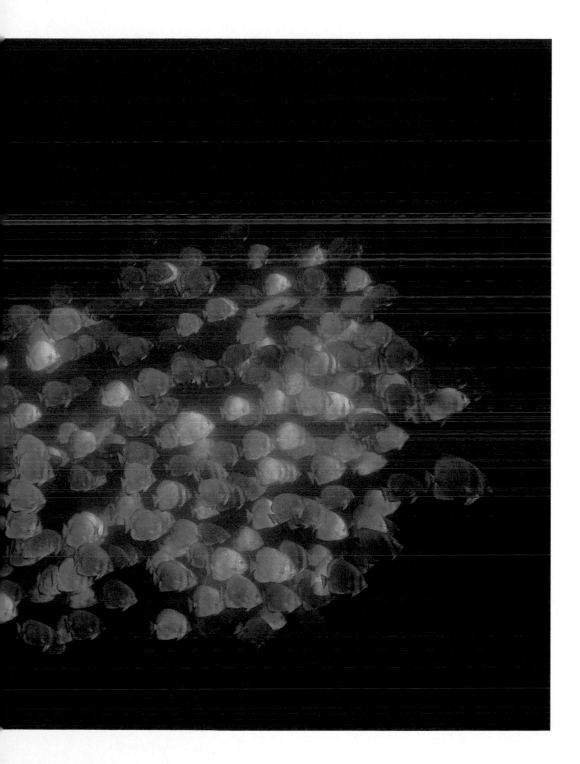

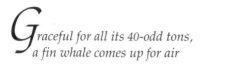

*Graceful for all its 40-odd tons,
a fin whale comes up for air* *in the Gulf of California. Here cool
currents and ample nutrients*

support a rich biota that includes
more than 800 species of fish.

FLIP NICKLIN

*T*all agave and clustered prickly pear flourish in the desert of Baja California, where an

© FRANS LANTING

astonishing variety of cacti and other plants represents a victory of life over aridity.

COOL TEMPERATE COASTS:

Realms of Mist and Marvels

By Jennifer C. Urquhart

ands move quickly, wielding sharp blades, cutting strips of bright red flesh into neat chunks. Others tuck the pieces into mason jars or seal the lids. A pressure cooker blasts away in the corner of the cluttered cabin. Jokes, soft laughter, conversation mingle with the clatter of glass and metal, but the pace never slackens. I'm at work too, packing the succulent salmon.

Outside, the Yakoun River flows softly by. All up and down the bank, Haida families work in their fishing camps. Narrow strips of salmon dangle on drying poles like so many red socks. A splash and a silvery glint signal another salmon in the net. A joyful shout greets each one. Bright sunlight polishes each blade of riffling grass. Spruce trees, gaunt, draped in lichens, punctuate the open expanse. A bald eagle soars overhead and lands clumsily on a snag. A raven cries a raucous demand to no one in particular. The inky dark water of the incoming tide reflects everything.

"It's magical here, magical," Robert Davidson murmurs, drawing his knife across another strip of fish. During most of the year he finds other uses for his hands at his home near Vancouver, British Columbia, where he is a distinguished painter-sculptor. But each summer he and his family spend a few weeks at their fishing camp in Haida Gwaii, the Queen Charlotte Islands. He grew up here, and these weeks are very special. It's for salmon to last the winter, of course, Robert tells me, but more to take him back to his Haida heritage.

For millennia the Haida—and other tribes—thrived in elaborate villages by the Pacific, developing a culture that distinguished this northwest coast of North America. Capt. John Meares, who sailed past in 1788, was astonished by one dwelling: "The trees that supported the roof . . . would render the mast of a first rate man of war diminutive. . . ." Beautifully crafted sea-going dugouts

Morning's low tide narrows the waters of
Canada's Queen Charlotte Islands and maroons
a triad of sea stars, ravenous predators.

DEWITT JONES

astounded such visitors as they swarmed out around the sailing ships.

Three figures atop a carved pole, the Watchmen, guarded many a Haida village. One looked down the coast, another up, the third toward the water. None faced the land. Though the terrain was rugged, coastal forests provided game and berries for the villages, as well as cedar and other useful materials. But mostly these people turned to the sea, skillfully harvesting its bounty of fish and the marine life they termed "beach food." They grew no crops, and needed none. "The tide is out and our table is set," the Tlingit say.

The salmon retains an almost sacred character in life and culture, here where forest meets ocean. Traditionally, coastal peoples welcomed back the First Salmon each year with honor and song as if it were a visiting chief; they reverently returned the bones to the water after eating it. Skewered and grilled the traditional way over an alder fire, the salmon I shared with the Davidsons was delicious. Over dinner they told me about the Haida social system. Custom divides people between two moieties, the Eagle and the Raven. Robert is of the Eagle, so tradition required that his wife, Dorothy, come from the Raven. Raven is the trickster, the clever one, sneaky—or so Eagle would say.

In early June, the sun was still lingering at 11 p.m. when I finally set out across a tidal marsh on my way back to town. I suddenly found myself mired knee-deep to the top of my gumboots in black gunk—hopelessly stuck. I yelled for help, imagining myself a relic in this latter-day La Brea tar pit, to be unearthed thousands of years from now by some curious paleontologist. Benjamin Davidson, age 13, came to the rescue. He hauled me onto firm ground. Then, with the tip of an oar, he dug my boots free. Why hadn't somebody warned me? "We *never* thought anyone would step into that stuff," came a laughter-choked reply. Raven, the trickster, must have been chuckling too.

Mild and moist of climate, this cool temperate zone offers one of the most agreeable and prolonged of journeys, one of the grandest. For naturalist John Muir, traveling a century ago, it provided a spectacle that challenged even his eloquence. "Never before this," he wrote in the north, "had I been embosomed in scenery so hopelessly beyond description." In places I would find that beauty as wild and pristine as it ever was. And more than skin deep. Sea and forest make this one of the most productive coastal regions in the world, and one of the longest. Stretching for hundreds of miles, it carries through northern California's forested fog belt and the broad sandy beaches that scallop the rocky coast of Oregon and Washington. It runs largely unbroken north to the Canadian border. In British Columbia it turns into a maze of islands and fjords, encompassing 16,000 miles of shore. Counting hundreds more islands, Alaska's Panhandle adds another 13,000 miles.

How such a productive region evolved is a complex story of geologic forces, of ocean currents and prevailing winds. I learned some of that story on the west coast of Vancouver Island. I strolled along a six-mile strand in Pacific Rim National Park and saw enormous logs and stumps, bleached white, strewn like giant matchsticks. The waves that had brought them rolled on in endless, rhythmic succession. Later I joined Bill McIntyre, the park's chief naturalist, and we boarded the cruiser *Dixie IV* to explore a little.

"This ocean is 'pacific' in name only," said Bill. The largest of the world's oceans, the Pacific sweeps 5,000 unbroken miles from Japan to North America. Prevailing winds take up moisture, then relinquish it on the high coastal mountains of the northwest; at the head of some fjords, rainfall exceeds 200 inches a year. Unimpeded, the winds foster huge swells. "One of the highest wave-energy areas in the world is along this coast—for frequency, duration, and magnitude," Bill said.

And what is the result of this turbulence? Crashing breakers mix air into the surf, and abundant oxygen supports marine life. Decomposed detritus full of nutrients settles to the continental shelf, a thousand feet down at most. Then upwelling comes into play. Bill pointed out, "It works like a 'nutrient pump.'" As strong summer winds out of the northwest generate drift currents in warm surface water, the earth's rotation shifts them offshore. Colder water wells up to replace warm. With it come nitrates and phosphates, to be stirred in the waves. These minerals nourish plankton. Tiny marine plants, phytoplankton, can flourish only in fairly shallow water that light can penetrate; and they're especially abundant off this coast.

Central as salmon may be in tradition and the local food chain, it is only one link. Haida myth, in fact, gives a key role to a lowly bivalve, a clam. Great Raven, the clever one, found the first men of his moiety cowering inside a huge clam shell on a beach and coaxed them out to enjoy the world. Women ascribe their beginning to the mollusks called chitons.

Dixie IV threaded the Broken Group, a confusion of small islands that resemble mountain fragments tossed willy-nilly into the sea. On them grew stunted trees twisted by the winds, but their lee gave us calm water. Half a dozen loons flashed by. A school of small coho salmon leaped and splashed, perhaps eluding a harbor porpoise. Bill pointed out bull kelp, which can grow 18 inches a day, and its gas-filled bladders that keep 15-foot-long blades near the surface and the light of day.

Fog, stormy weather, and complex currents and tides are more the rule than the exception here. About 125 major shipwrecks have given the area its sobriquet "Graveyard of the Pacific." Today its hazards could bring calamity to supertanker traffic. I noticed a large white structure high on a forested ridge, and Bill identified it: "It's a radar dome, part of the tracking system set up a few years ago to cope with supertankers along these treacherous shores. The system tracks the location of vessels over 20 feet long."

In December 1988 a barge off Washington State had spilled a quarter of a million gallons of heavy oil; within two weeks its oil had reached the Vancouver Island region, including a small island where we went ashore. Much of the thick black gunk had been removed. "It basically comes down to plastic bags and hands," Bill said, "to gather chunks of congealed oil and dead seabirds so they won't contaminate the food chain. We collected 3,000 birds, but there were probably ten times more killed." We stopped at a small rocky beach left untouched so specialists could monitor any natural dispersal.

"It's not always easy to tell which is oil," Bill remarked, digging a pocket-knife into a soft black area: oil, an inch thick in places, sticky to the touch. He pointed to a broad band of black near the splash zone. "That's *Verrucaria*, a kind of lichen that survives just at the high tide line." It proved to be dry, and rough. Other black patches lay well below the lichen band. "Tar spot. It's a mimic alga that covers rocks at a certain tide level. Feels slippery, but it's not oil." Clearly, successful oil cleanups require a well-trained crew. "It's a slow process, but there are bacteria that eat oil," said Bill. "They are really pigging out these days!" The disastrous oil spill of the *Exxon Valdez* in March 1989 was on everyone's mind, although it occurred more than 1,200 miles to the northwest in Prince William Sound, Alaska.

Oil notwithstanding, we saw a bewildering variety of seaweeds in the tidal zone. Bright green sea lettuce resembles its leafy namesake and indeed is edible. Turkish towel also earns its name; it's harvested, dried, and sold as a backscrub. So do seersucker algae, puckery stuff.

Hiking into the forest, we reached a mossy open area where terraced middens of seashells record the presence of Indian villagers over the centuries. Bill pointed out a cedar with bark stripped long ago. "The native people took bark from the north side. Fewer branches, therefore fewer knots. The women used different widths to weave mats, bark clothing—any number of useful objects. Here the natives always left some bark on the tree so as not to kill it and offend its guardian or spirit."

Compared to the shifting sands of a barrier island, these rocky shores appear immutable. But change comes here too. Waves and storms constantly bash cliffs, sea stacks, and boulders, wearing them down by imperceptible degrees until a rock face sloughs off or a stack topples into the sea.

In other ways change is coming with startling speed, as I saw on a flight north from Vancouver to the Queen Charlotte Islands. A jumble of snow-capped peaks lay inland; near-vertical slopes of the Coast Mountains plunged into surf. Although many kept their blanket of dark coniferous forest, loggers are transforming the region into an immense tree farm. Enormous swaths, recently clear-cut, exposed the mountains' massive bones to the sky; along shore, far below, rafts of logs dotted the dark blue water. Such extensive logging does not come without controversy. Of all disputed issues, logging would be the one I encountered most often along these wild shores. A low-altitude floatplane trip across the Queen Charlottes gave me a keener sense of the stakes. In cutover blocks, barren slide areas streaked the slopes and logging roads spread widening patterns of erosion. At the southern end of Moresby Island, slated to become a national park, forests still stand untouched. And here I joined a holiday party on the 32-foot charter cruiser *Kingii*. Two whiskery faces—harbor seals—popped up in a tangle of kelp to watch me go aboard.

Huge old trees, covered with moss and lichen, formed bowers for our tents onshore. A small black-tailed doe browsed by my tent. We watched the lingering sunset and listened to the flute song of a hermit thrush. Black oyster-catchers sped low across the water. They were fast becoming my favorite birds, comical creatures with ungainly pink feet and absurdly large red bills shaped like an oysterman's knife. Once a great squawking and ruffling of feathers caught our attention, and an ornithologist in the crew explained the somewhat chaotic domestic arrangements of the species. One parent goes off duty at the nest and the other takes over, with a little marital bickering.

"Our boat's name is Haida for 'Always-looking-down-into-the-sea,' " Charlotte Husband told me the next morning. And that was our intention as we headed out in a dinghy with Charlotte's spouse, Terry. We planned to find dinner, in the form of rock scallops, and examine a flourishing world between sea and land.

"It is a fantastic jungle, mad in a Lewis Carroll sort of way," wrote biologist Rachel Carson, describing such an intertidal zone. "For what proper jungle, twice every twenty-four hours begins to sag lower and lower and finally lies prostrate for several hours, only to rise again?"

Indeed, at low tide fronds of sea palms and rockweed had collapsed over the rocks we approached. Armed with screwdriver and bucket, Terry set out confidently. "It's like looking for Easter eggs. I did this when I was really little around here," he said, spotting a specimen that matched his grasp.

Appropriately in a Lewis Carroll world, creatures here are a little odd. As the scallop fed on microorganisms, its orange mantle beamed between open shells like a big Cheshire cat smile. Instead of a toothy grin, little beady eyes peered out along the edges of the "lips." Terry deftly pried the creature from its crevice and dropped it into the bucket. The scallop clamped shut, the smile all gone. And I, like Alice's Walrus, sympathized with the beleaguered bivalve—though I anticipated a fine meal. Terry assuaged my guilt: By taking only the larger, older scallops, he needs fewer to make a meal. This leaves more of the young ones to reproduce their kind.

Through crystalline waters Charlotte and I peered into a world colorful enough to rival a coral reef: rosy pink coralline algae; sea anemones, some with thick scarlet stalks, others large and green and reminiscent of a Van Gogh chrysanthemum. Pencil-thin calcareous tube worms with red tentacles like a fern bouquet. Abalones; turban snails; bright sea slugs; dark chitons, primitive rugged-looking creatures also called "gumboots." A brilliant galaxy of sea stars in purples, oranges, reds—with names like sunflower, bat, leather; fiercely armed sea urchins in purple or green or red. A foot-long sea cucumber, maroon with bright orange protuberances, endured our handling without incident. Some of this family, if molested, simply disgorge their innards—and if the attacker is distracted or deterred, new organs will regenerate by and by.

All along the northwest coast, tides have quirks of their own, which create a broad range of ecological niches. On any given day the two high tides vary substantially in height, as do the two lows. And depending on the phase of the moon, there are also biweekly extremes of high and low. Thus some tidal zones are seldom exposed to air, others seldom wet.

On a treeless islet, Charlotte and I clambered ashore across slippery mounds of seaweed and onto the rocks. The world came alive with birds—very active birds—for we had come upon a nesting island for gulls and oystercatchers. The gulls seemed unflustered; but the oystercatchers, with their customary lack of restraint, hovered and dived and squawked at us in apparent hysteria. We retreated to the boat, stepping carefully to avoid the nests, only to blunder almost immediately into another nursery. Seals atop an offshore rock eyed us warily, then slid into the water and away. But one stayed near, bobbing up and down only a few feet from us. Then we heard her gentle barking call as she coaxed her days-old pup to follow her into the water.

We camped that evening in forest at the edge of a narrow rocky beach. As the sun lowered to the west, mountains flattened into two-dimensional layers of rose and gray against a pink-vermeil sky. The scallops, delicately sautéed in butter with wild mushrooms, made a delicious meal. Soon we had eaten them up, every one.

Wilder shores lay farther to the north, and I watched them from a larger vessel, the big ferry *Taku* that plies the Inside Passage along the coast of British Columbia and Alaska. These sheltered waters offered views of undisturbed shores. At land's edge grew conifers spar-straight in martial lines, and behind them rose snow-covered peaks with glaciers for epaulets. The ferry plowed steadily on, the water shirring softly as salt met air.

We called at Ketchikan in midafternoon. With about 7,400 residents, this is Alaska's fifth largest city. The settled area stretches for about 30 miles along the coast, crammed against a wall of mountains. Once a gold-rush town, now a logging and fishing center, it has its own wildness of a roughneck sort.

Even so, John Muir's comment still rang true: ". . . we seemed to float in true fairyland. . . ." Next morning the scene before us was growing ever more precipitous. I leaned over the rail inhaling air so crisp and fresh it seemed to sing. Dolphins cavorted in our wake. Muir had found special charm in the myriad islands that dot these waters: ". . . they seemed detached beauties, like extracts from a poem. . . . their beauty is the beauty of youth. . . ."

By the time we passed east of Admiralty, a much larger island, bald eagles were commonplace. I saw them as dark silhouettes soaring high, and as white dots against the dark conifers at the water's edge. On the mainland, glaciers flowed slowly down high slopes while their iceberg offspring floated in the calm water of fjords and inlets.

Juneau, Alaska's capital, a city of 25,000, has glaciers too. But it was the mountainside forests of spruce and hemlock, a splendid backdrop for the city, that I sought. As in British Columbia, logging is a contentious issue in Alaska, and the outcome of this quarrel will shape the future of these shores. No less than 80 percent of southeast Alaska lies within the Tongass National Forest— almost 17 million acres of public land. The key word for this issue and this region is old-growth.

By bureaucratic definition, old-growth timber is anything older than 150 or 200 years. Technically, much of the Tongass qualifies; but much of that consists of scrubby, low-quality trees. The logging companies don't want those. They want the prime groves, the huge trees—500 or 800 years old, some of them— that flourish in temperate rain forests along the coast or in creek bottoms. But these areas, I learned, are the very ones essential to wildlife—eagles, bears, deer—and to fishery habitat as well.

Near Juneau, one morning, I joined Matt Kirchhoff, a biologist with the Alaska Department of Fish and Game. He has been studying old-growth ecology, concentrating on the Sitka black-tailed deer, and worries about what will happen to wildlife populations if the big trees are cut: "Most of the eagles nest in the larger trees—older than 400 years, and within 300 feet of the shore."

We hiked up a trail into a tract first logged in the 1950s. Dense stands of Sitka spruce, all about 30 feet high, grew so thick we couldn't have squeezed between the trunks. There was little room for undergrowth and hardly any light to sustain it. "There's nothing good here for the deer—or for anything else," said Matt, "except maybe porcupines and a few songbirds that come after bugs. You've got a lot of forage here after a stand's first cut." He pointed to tiny bunchberries and other small herbaceous plants in the sunlit corridor of the trail. "But in this part of the world it's unavailable to the animals in the wintertime, because of the deep snow cover. Then the canopy closes and there is nothing for the next 80 or 120 years."

We came to a vantage point on the trail. "See that stand of trees just ahead of us—it's very even-age, about 65 years old. It's not aesthetically unattractive, not like a newly clear-cut slope. That's one of the ironies. The worst possible stage of the forest regrowth—for wildlife—doesn't really look bad. From the ferry, the cruise ship, the airplane, even standing here, it looks fine.

"It's like a one-way ratchet," Matt concluded. "There is always going to be economic pressure to get into the valuable stands of trees; and once they're gone, they're gone. It's a rare and unique ecosystem. We tend to lose sight of that. Over centuries you get this dynamic steady state where individual trees are growing up and dying, creating gaps where young trees grow up. There is no amount of management or silviculture manipulation that is going to bring back old-growth forests."

Two bumper stickers I saw spoke bluntly to the logging issue. One, in Ketchikan: "More Jobs Not More Wilderness." Another, in Juneau: "Cut the Crap, Save the Old-Growth." In fact, the U.S. Forest Service had awarded 50-year contracts for logging in the Tongass because it hoped to create a stable industry and maintain jobs—although the cost to the taxpayer runs high. I met a commercial fisherman, however, who pointed out that fishing employs more people in southeast Alaska than logging does.

This was Gordon Williams, a native of Juneau but now, in his thirties, a resident of Angoon, a village on Admiralty Island. We discussed his trade at his home, the evening before he set out for three days of salmon fishing. "If you're from Ohio, say, and you know nothing of fish, you think fish are in the ocean and trees are on the land. You don't really understand why cutting a tree five miles up a stream would hurt your salmon. You don't know the life cycle of the salmon. But the commercial fishing industry here is very dependent upon wise management of the Tongass, as it provides the bulk of the spawning and rearing habitat for our five species of Pacific salmon. And tideland areas provide essential habitat for our shellfish stocks."

Gordy doesn't object to all logging. "It's the unfortunate quirk of nature that the biggest trees and the fish habitat and the deer habitat are all in the same place—the river valleys, the watersheds." He doesn't want those disrupted. He referred to a Tlingit saying that he recalled as "Come visit us, we will share our food with you, just don't break the dish." Gordy fears that logging policies are "putting some irreparable cracks in that dish."

Most of Angoon's 620 residents are Tlingit, and seem to like its isolation. A ferry calls three times a week; not long ago Tlingit leaders vetoed the construction of an airport. Matthew J. Fred, Sr., the traditional cultural leader, works for the Forest Service and told me with pride about his tribe's decision to protect the lands where they live. Areas designated for Angoon under the Alaska National Interest Lands Conservation Act will be reserved for subsistence use and recreation as part of the national monument that includes most of the million acres of Admiralty. "We're natural born conservationists," Matthew says. (That may be a little overstated; tribal lands elsewhere are being logged heavily.)

We strolled at waterside, and I noticed basketball trophies gleaming on windowsills in small frame houses. Lanky boys and girls jogged past, in training for the season. Matthew showed me more traditional structures, clan houses with such names as Raven Bone House, Shark House, Killer Whale Tooth House. "Long ago," he said, "during the potlatch—or party—to dedicate the Killer Whale Fin House, killer whales came in. We threw berries into the water for them. The creator made the killer whale out of cedar. Killer whale fat and cedar sound exactly the same when they burn."

Like the Haida, the Tlingit recognize Eagle and Raven moieties. In reality, as well, these birds seem to share the world at Angoon. To the raven and his little brother, the crow, belong the morning, which they fill with coarse squabbling. Late afternoon brings the more lyrical notes of the eagle as it swoops down to feed. Eagles spend much of the day perched quietly in waterside trees. But one morning I watched an eagle dive for a fish and then swim awkwardly to shore, its wings too wet for flight. And one evening a pair engaged in a spectacular courtship dance, whirling in the sunlit air with their talons locked.

Northwest of Admiralty, in Icy Strait, run swift waters where herring and other schooling fish abound. Larger fish and marine mammals flourish here too. In summer humpback whales gather to feed. Early one rainy morning I joined a party of kayakers for several days. Six of us cruised near Chichagof Island in three sleek double kayaks. Cutting through the water, I felt a kinship with native boatmen observed by a British naval officer hereabouts in 1788—"paddling and singing with all the Jollity imaginable . . . to all appearances as waterproof as ducks. . . ." We weren't singing yet, but we could compete with ducks in our layers of waterproof gear and our kayak skirts.

With guide Lisa McLaren, I paddled quietly through beds of bull and giant kelp. Sometimes I could only slap at the surface with my paddle, the tangle of kelp was so thick. Seals popped up now and again for a look at our flotilla. "It's great in a kayak," said Lisa, who had lived in Alaska for 13 years. "You feel like you are the first person ever to see a place—well, maybe the second!"

Sometimes we skimmed through clear water inside the kelp beds. Once a couple of sea lions swam near. Then, out in the strait, two humpback whales surfaced blowing spray high into the air with a great whooshing blast, loud as the air brakes on an 18-wheeler. We paddled closer to watch. With an easy grace incredible in creatures 40 to 50 feet long, the whales leaped and rolled. Named *Megaptera*, "large-winged," for its very long flippers, the humpback uses those fins for all sorts of acrobatic maneuvers. Finally tail flukes flipped a salute our way, slapped a sharp report, and disappeared. Until the turn of the century perhaps 15,000 humpbacks lived in the North Pacific. Only about 1,000 survived the depredations of whaling. As many as 15 or so feed here in summer; other pods pass through on occasion.

Bam . . . bam . . . bam. . . . It resounded again and again, like artillery firing a 6 a.m. bombardment. Bright sunlight was filtering into my tent as I came to, slowly, with a twinge of anxiety. Had war broken out? Not at all. It was simply the humpbacks breaching—flinging 35-ton bodies out of the water and landing with a boom to vie with a cannon's roar. No one really knows why the whales do this. But it certainly provides a sure-fire wake-up call.

Seals and sea lions seemed to lead the way as we paddled westward later in the morning. That night we camped on a beach terrace thick with rye grass and delicate shooting stars and strawberry flowers. Waking next morning to a spirited tapping of rain on the tents, we got a leisurely start to the day.

After breakfast we followed a bear trail in the dripping woods. Our leader, Judy Brakel, pointed out some bear droppings and a set of paw prints in the damp earth—large prints. These bears are the huge browns, a color variant of the grizzly, that fatten on spawning salmon along the northwest coast; the Tlingit name for Admiralty Island, in fact, is Kootznoowoo, "brown bear fort island," for a population of roughly one bear per square mile. Staring down at the trail, we saw only one set of tracks. "Brown bears tend to walk in the same tracks over and over," Judy remarked. We didn't expect to encounter bears near shore; it would be later in the summer when the spawning salmon and the ripening berries would bring them down from the high muskeg country.

Plants of the forest and shore also interest Judy. She had us sample twisted stalk, also called wild cucumber because of the flavor, and later we learned that the slender leaves of goose tongue are delicious stir-fried. She singled out devil's club, which I had clutched by mistake scrambling up a bank; I got a handful of prickles. Peeling away the spines on a stalk of it, she revealed a green interior bark used by native peoples of the region to treat infections.

Later we cruised along shore under a clearing sky. Squalls passed to the west like gossamer curtains, veiling and then revealing small islands with mountains beyond. Brants swam by quietly. Scoters took off at our approach, their wings squeaking like a chorus of loose fanbelts. Once four sea otters invited us to play, rolling over and spinning around, swimming on their backs with paws up and looking in our direction. Three of them followed us almost to shore and seemed disappointed when we splashed in to camp.

Ending our trip, returning on a motor cruiser across Icy Strait, we found our whales again, still cavorting and feeding. A hydrophone lowered into the water picked up a gentle and mournful wail that touched deep into us all. Unwilling to speak, we listened to their song—the song of kindred souls that seem to link us with ocean waters, waters so filled with life and from whence life came. I hoped they would always be here to sing to us.

FOLLOWING PAGES: An acrobatic duo of orcas, or killer whales, breaches in salmon-filled summer waters off Canada's Vancouver Island.

JOHN K.B. FORD

More at home under rock ledges or on the sea floor crunching crabs and scallops, a giant octopus—five feet long—propels itself through sunlit waters in the Strait of Georgia. On the wilder, western side of Vancouver Island (right), a notorious graveyard of ships, waves pummel a jagged shore in Pacific Rim National Park.

FOLLOWING PAGES: Dotted with pearly spines, a purple sea star—one of nearly 100 species in the Strait of Georgia—inches its way through algae.

© DAVID DOUBILET (ABOVE); STEVEN C. WILSON / ENTHEOS (OPPOSITE); © DAVID DOUBILET (FOLLOWING PAGES)

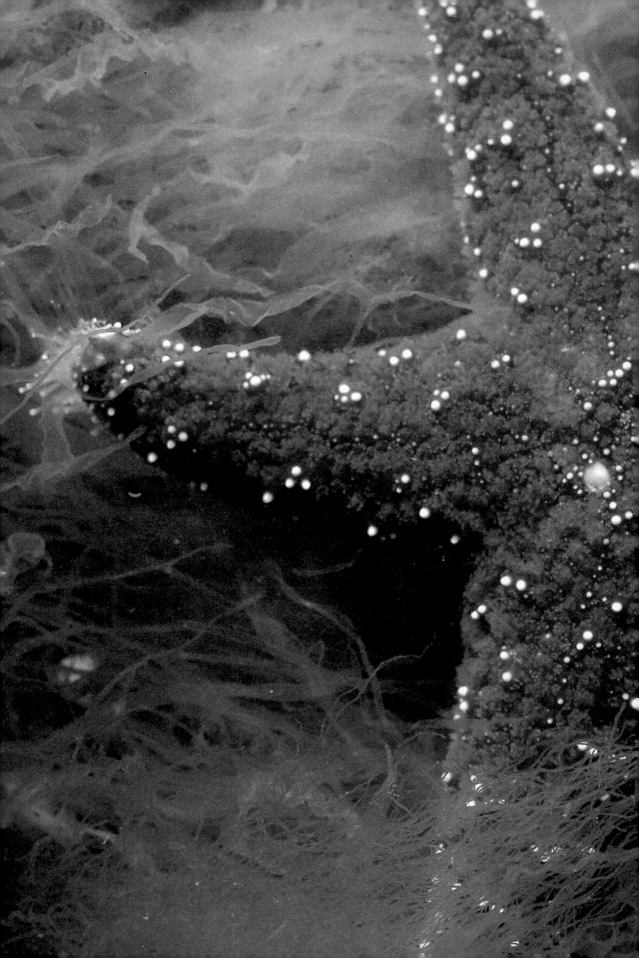

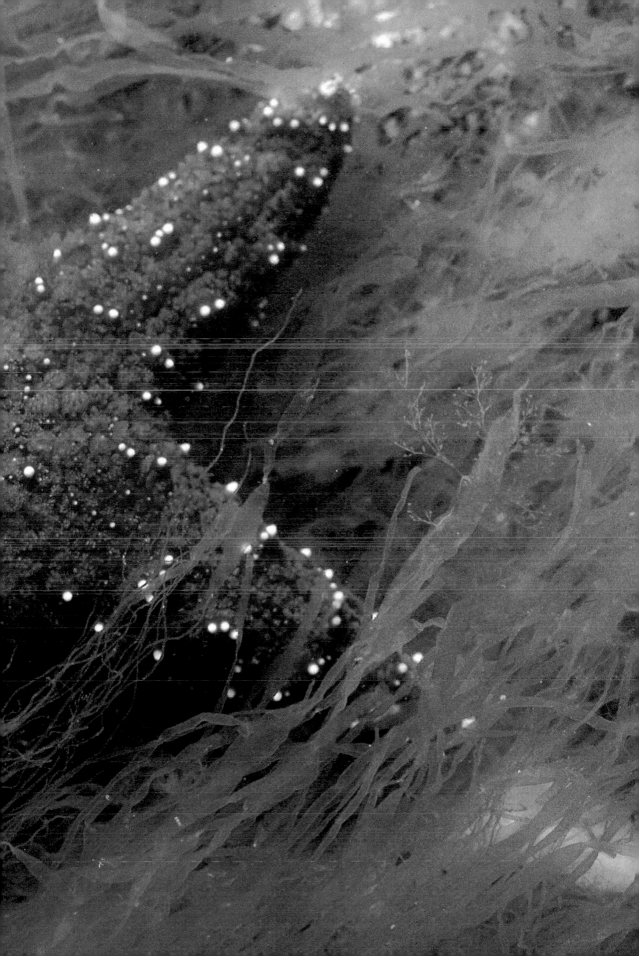

Adding human music to the sounds of wind and sea, a tradition-conscious Haida Indian chants and drums on a beach in the Queen Charlotte Islands. A stylized bear's head decorates his long tunic; his blanket has the emblem of his clan, Raven. Famed as carvers of cedar totem poles and as skilled fishermen, the Haida have inhabited the 150-isle archipelago for 10,000 years or more. At its northern end, the tip of Langara Island (right) looks toward the Alaska Panhandle.

FOLLOWING PAGES: A bald eagle—Chief of the Sky Beings, says Haida legend—takes flight in a misty forest. The Charlottes have the highest density of bald eagle nests in all of Canada.

DeWITT JONES (ABOVE, LEFT, AND FOLLOWING PAGES)

137

Glaciers past and present leave their
mark on the rugged coast of southeastern
Alaska. An eagle rests at the apex of a
berg calved from a tidewater glacier
(below) in the Tracy Arm-Fords Terror
Wilderness, part of the Tongass
National Forest. During the Ice Age,
glaciers widened the coastal valleys;
afterward, rising sea level drowned the
gorges, creating fjords. In the fjord called
Fords Terror (right), fog and forest blanket
the ice-scoured 1,000-foot walls.

TOM BEAN (ABOVE AND OPPOSITE); PAUL CHESLEY / PHOTOGRAPHERS ASPEN (FOLLOWING PAGES)

FOLLOWING PAGES: Who will believe them,
the kayakers must wonder, when they tell
of a humpback whale diving not 30 feet away.

COOL TEMPERATE COASTS:

A Portfolio

Magnificent forests cloak wild coastlines in the cool temperate region, growing prodigiously in the moderate summers and moist winters of this mid-latitude zone. Stands of old-growth timber—reduced because of logging—still exist on the southwest coasts of Chile and New Zealand and the Pacific Northwest coast of North America. This region includes about 2,000 miles of drizzly, wave-lashed coast from northern California through the Panhandle of south-eastern Alaska, near the 60th parallel; and here the world's tallest trees flourish. The famous coast redwoods reach heights of 350 feet in sheltered valleys, while 200-foot Sitka spruce blanket waterside mountain slopes.

"Marine west coast" is one label for this climate. Moist oceanic winds bring precipitation to such shores. Coastal mountain ranges exaggerate the effect; they act as rainmakers, forcing clouds to rise into cooler air and spill their moisture. Some coastal spots in the Pacific Northwest get more than 200 inches of rain a year, and rank among the wettest places on earth.

Cool temperate climate, with its mean annual temperatures of about 35° to 60°F, dominates much of western Europe. From northern Spain it extends north and east into the Baltic Sea; it includes the British Isles, and reaches its northernmost point in coastal Norway, above the Arctic Circle. Europe's great coastal forests were cut down centuries ago. Bogs and moors overlook the sea in western Ireland and Scotland, where strong winds would stunt any saplings and Ice Age glaciers scoured away old soils.

Those Pleistocene glaciers also created the fjords that lend drama to the coasts of Norway, Patagonia, New Zealand's South Island, and the Inside Passage of British Columbia and Alaska. Even today glaciers survive here, kept in being by the abundant snow that falls in the high coastal mountains.

Summer fogs and winter rains sustain a fern-carpeted grove of redwoods, coastal trees found only in California and southern Oregon.

CHARLES A. MAUZY

$\mathcal{D}$efenseless against the pounding Pacific surf, sea stacks slowly crumble on the weathered coast

© 1989 HARALD SUND

of Oregon. The craggy columns are all that remain of a headland that jutted out to sea.

*E*scaping stormy waters, Steller's sea lions mass inside Sea Lion Caves near Florence, Oregon.

This colony does not migrate; breeding takes place in summer on ledges outside the cavern.

RANDY WELLS / ALLSTOCK, INC.

*S*ea palms stand their ground under the assault of ocean waves at Cape Perpetua in Oregon. Cup-like fibers anchor these two-foot-high kelp plants to rocks in the intertidal zone; a hollow rubbery stipe, or stem, lets them bend with the heavy surf—adaptations to the high-energy coasts of the eastern Pacific. Waves build as high as 100 feet in winter on their trans-Pacific journey; at right, spindrift blows seaward as a swell crests in the shallows.

SCOTT BLACKMAN / TOM STACK & ASSOCIATES; STEVEN C. WILSON / ENTHEOS (LOWER LEFT)

During a rare cold snap, ebb tide strands slabs of ice on oyster-rich mud flats in Washington's

MATTHEW WILSON / ENTHEOS

tranquil Willapa Bay, one of the last estuaries in the Pacific Northwest without industrial pollution.

C *ollecting a traditional delicacy, a Maori woman pulls sea urchins off tide-bared rocks near*

JOHN EASTCOTT / YVA MOMATIUK

East Cape on New Zealand's North Island. The shallows also offer abundant shellfish.

POLAR COASTS:

The Last
and the Loneliest

By Tom Melham

Within the Antarctic Circle, wrote the first explorer to venture so far south, "the Sea is so pestered with ice, that the land is thereby inaccessible." By February 6, 1775, after months of search, Captain James Cook had concluded that any lands near the South Pole would "never be explored." Pack ice prevented him from sighting Antarctica, let alone setting foot on it, but he managed to sail around it safely despite countless gales in what would become known as the earth's stormiest sea. Its perils included thick fogs and snowstorms, cold that left ropes frozen "like wire, Sails like board or plates of Metal," and ice, gigantic bergs and ever-shifting floes.

Indeed, it was the region's overabundant ice that convinced Cook some unseen landmass lay to the south. He discovered the subantarctic island of South Georgia, no farther from the Equator than his own Yorkshire birthplace, and found it utterly unlike Britain in climate. "Who would have thought," he marveled, "that an Island . . . between the Latitude of 54° and 55°, should in the very height of Summer be in a manner wholly covered many fathoms deep with frozen Snow. . . ." He was sure that winter ice formed here "which in the Spring is broke off and dispersed over the Sea. . . ." Even so, he reasoned, this island could not produce a ten-thousandth part of the ice he had seen; only a continent or "large tract of land" could account for such "vast floats."

Later explorers would prove him right. A continental Antarctic did exist, as geographers had predicted since classical antiquity. It turned out to be almost half again as large as the United States; a heat sink; a land of extremes; a brutal, vast white hole far more memorable for its lacks than for its offerings. Alone of all the continents, it had never harbored an indigenous human population.

Black-browed albatrosses and other seabirds
nest on the tussocky slopes of South Georgia, ice-free
summer breeding grounds for Antarctic species.

© FRANS LANTING

Antarctica is the coldest, driest, windiest, wildest, starkest, and loneliest of the earth's continents. Also the highest, and with the least stable margins. A colossal ice cap—more than two miles thick in places—blankets 98 percent of it year-round. Most of the shore lies icebound even in summertime; in winter the ice cover more than doubles in area, encasing perhaps 12 million square miles—an expanse larger than Africa. Observed by time-lapse camera from space, such changes can seem the pulsings of the earth's great white heart. In fact, Antarctica functions like a global pump; it drives atmospheric and oceanic circulation patterns, thus influencing weather worldwide.

The Arctic ice cap also pulses seasonally, though less dramatically. It expands while the Antarctic cap shrinks, for arctic and austral seasons are reversed. Both Poles receive only glancing blows of sunlight, never the steady solar barrage of the tropics. Both Poles endure six-month winter "nights" and six-month summer "days." Yet they are more opposites than equals. The Arctic is fairly shallow sea fringed by landmasses: the continual mixing of waters moderates its climate and leaves the cloak of ice relatively thin. In Antarctica, however, snows built up over millennia nurture a permanent ice sheet. This reflects sunlight, further chilling the region. Antarctic ice represents three-quarters of the world's fresh water, yet most of the area is desert, its moisture so locked up by extreme cold that blizzards more often involve snow blowing from place to place than snow falling from the skies.

In many ways the last continent is our planet's closest approximation to outer space: empty, silent, frigid. Temperatures here have dipped as low as -129.6°F, colder than parts of Mars. These frozen wastes possess an alien, other-worldly feel; black and white dominate a minimalist spectrum ruled by rock, ice, and very little else. Soils hardly exist. No trees or shrubs soften the cobbled scapes; apart from two species of grass on the Antarctic Peninsula, lichens and mosses represent the largest, most advanced, and most varied native plants. The biggest terrestrial animals are all but invisible: midges a sixth of an inch long. Antarctica shelters no native land mammals; no reptiles; no amphibians. It is stunning in its bleakness, almost too wild for wildlife.

But then there is the great southern ocean, encircling this nearly sterile ice-desert with one of the richest concentrations of marine life anywhere. Though species are few compared to the numbers in warmer waters, populations can be immense. Dr. David Parmelee, a University of Minnesota professor with 13 seasons of Antarctic experience, explains:

"You'll find more niches—more habitats for different species—on one tree in the Amazon rain forest than on vast reaches of the Antarctic." Environmental rigors limit biological diversity here, in the water and on land. "Plants and animals have to adapt. Not many can. Those that have, have been very successful. The southern ocean is very, very rich."

Its species range from microscopic diatoms to multi-ton blue whales, largest of all creatures. They include phytoplankton, hydroids, ice algae, kelp, starfish, and squid, as well as icefish with natural antifreezes in their blood.

In addition to such curiosities, Antarctic seas contain small crustaceans known as *Euphausia superba*, or krill. Krill probably number in the trillions; their biomass has been estimated at 100 to 700 million tons, the high figure roughly ten times man's annual harvest of other seafood worldwide. Directly or indirectly, krill support almost all other Antarctic animals, including the trademark penguins, seals, and seabirds that come ashore in the tens of millions. So it is that the ocean nurtures land's edge as well as itself, spawning a prolific coastal ecosystem far livelier than the continent's bleak core.

Marine influences abound along the Antarctic Peninsula, a mountainous tail of ice and islands curving gently north from the roughly circular continent. Its tip lies only 600 miles from southernmost South America. Flanked by moderating sea, it boasts some of Antarctica's richest biology and mildest weather. In January, average temperatures rise above freezing point. Travelers have nicknamed it the region's "Banana Belt" or "Riviera." Indeed, there are places here where the seemingly nonstop winds fall off and sunbathing in summer's long rays of light becomes possible, even truly enjoyable. Even so, the peninsula looks denuded: Its sea stacks and volcanic cliffs and repetitive scree slopes create a gravel-pit image, edged in ever-present ice. Arriving here from South America, I felt like Dorothy as she returns from Oz to Kansas—and the movie screen abruptly switches from full color to black and white. This land and its wildlife are drawn in monochrome.

Antarctica remains one of the earth's less frequented ports of call. Over the past two or three decades, no more than 50,000 or 60,000 people have visited its shores: fewer than attend a single Super Bowl game. Those who do come, however, tend to return. John Hall, base commander of Great Britain's Rothera Station on Adelaide Island halfway down the peninsula, has spent part of every year but one since 1973 in the vicinity.

"There is a magic to the place," he explains. "It's empty in many ways and yet full in others. There's nothing so special as to be in the middle of a penguin rookery when it's midnight by the clock and the sun is still bright, the sky is beautiful, the birds busy with their routine, fairly oblivious to your presence. It's lovely to be able to go very close to animals without them being afraid, without them knowing really what you are or who you are."

Their lack of fear stems largely from Antarctica's total lack of land predators (except for man). It's especially impressive because the animals are so gregarious. I remember one rookery, a flattish islet only a few hundred yards wide, just off the coast of Adelaide. From a mile away it seemed an abstraction, whitish rocks scrolled with a black, wandering maze of swirls and blobs that ballooned into peninsulas here and narrowed down to nothing there. Half a mile closer, the patterns resolved into thousands upon thousands of black dots, packing some areas as densely as rush-hour riders fill a subway, yet leaving others curiously empty. A faint nonstop burbling, like a distant generator, came to my ears. Breezes carried the unmistakable ammonia odor of guano. The dots, of course, were penguins—an estimated 100,000 I was told—mostly Adélies, with some chinstraps. Awkward and slow on land, the birds are remarkably strong and adept swimmers, bursting from the sea like champagne corks to land on an iceberg or on a rock ledge. Thousands of them crowded this one insignificant rock. It was January, the austral summer: breeding time.

Offshore, icebergs cruised chunky buttermilk seas—some ponderous and dull as battleships, others glowing with cloud-filtered light or pinnacled like a Mormon tabernacle. Snow petrels, pigeon-shaped and pure white except for their black eyes and beaks, roved the coast in wavy lines. Though all traveled the same direction, each bird took its own route, skimming waves or soaring up to dance among iceberg spires. These were no labored, gullish flappers, no rigid formation fliers, but pure aerialists out for fun. Again and again they passed, rising and skewing and plummeting and plainly in love with the air. Then southern fulmars joined in, the black edges of their white wings catching the sunlight with a flickering, stop-action effect. They flew much as tropical fish swim: in loose, fluttery shoals. The leader turned one way, suddenly another, and the billowing pack followed, seeming less a group of individuals than one dynamic, pulsing amoeba making its protoplasmic way across the sky. Below them Weddell and fur seals snoozed on sun-drenched cobbles, while offshore other creatures roamed unseen. So much life on Adelaide's coast, yet go inland only half a mile or so, up the sloping ice beyond this narrow shore, and you abruptly enter the Void.

It is blindingly white on clear days, each crystal of the ice crust glistening separately, as with inner fire. Crevasses slash the surface, their blue, icicled interiors soothing and dreamlike to sunblazed eyes. Ahead, glaciered mountains rise from snowfields unmarked by man. Behind, more snowcapped peaks loom from the southern horizon, each col and ridge so clearly defined they seem only a two-day hike away—until a map is brought out, showing them a hundred miles distant. The air's daunting transparency is its own applause.

In heavier weather, mirages can dog Antarctic visitors. Inverted icebergs drape the sky, clouds masquerade as bulwarks of land, bergs seem islands, landmarks below the horizon magically draw near. Today, however, no such tricks intrude. Adelaide's white interior stands beautiful, pure, clean—but sterile. No seals or penguins venture here, no petrels play overhead. There are no visible life-forms at all. Not even a skua, the ubiquitous scavenger and bird of prey, bothers to follow. You hear no sounds but the wind. Just half a mile from the sea, yet the lines are sternly drawn; Antarctic life seems tightly bound to the coasts.

Actually, a few seabirds—mostly the smaller petrels—venture inland to breed, nesting in scree or in mountaintop crevices that hide them from aerial predators. But not here, not today; prolific shores and vacant ice present an all-or-nothing panorama. This coastal ecosystem has sharply defined limits; life is always precarious. Vast, seemingly infinite populations do not guarantee survival, not even in such a remote location. Brutal though Antarctica may be to man, it has proven vulnerable to his touch.

Whalers and sealers took immense, ill-recorded numbers of animals from Antarctic waters in the 19th and early 20th centuries. Fur seals have made a comeback since commercial sealing collapsed. Whaling, mainly by Japan, continues today, though on a much reduced scale. Most whale species are now protected, but some already may have run out of time. Also, Soviet and Eastern Bloc fishing fleets have reduced certain fishes, of a family commonly called Antarctic cod, to non-harvestable levels. Krill are being taken, for human consumption and for a protein-rich chicken feed: about 500,000 tons annually.

"We haven't overfished krill yet," says Dr. Langdon Quetin, a research biologist at the University of California's Marine Science Institute, in Santa Barbara. "But it's a very important animal. It's the dominant source of food for top predators, and the ecosystem is much more complex than originally thought. You're harvesting at an intermediate level of the food chain; it's hard to say what the effects will be."

Dr. Dieter Müller, a West German phycologist, agrees: "It's important to know how long it takes the biomass to replace itself. This isn't known; it could take years. Just because there have been huge standing crops doesn't mean such yields are sustainable year after year."

Quetin adds that the Japanese have developed a taste for gravid female krill, those carrying eggs. If trawlers begin to focus on such females, harvests would deplete succeeding generations as well as the current one.

I n addition to its living resources, Antarctica may possess valuable mineral deposits. It contains huge reserves of low-grade coal, perhaps the world's largest, as well as indications of petroleum, natural gas, and strategic metals. Increasingly it sparks international interest, and political maneuvering. For one thing, no one owns it. In this century seven nations have laid claim to portions of it—overlapping claims in some cases, with the added riddle of whether to classify permanent coastal ice shelves as land for legal purposes. These nations and others, however, abide by the Antarctic Treaty. In 1961 the treaty set aside such claims and dedicated the continent to peaceful and scientific purposes. But as supplies of food and minerals dwindle elsewhere, pressures to exploit this last repository will increase. Any development promises to affect coastal areas in particular, since ports will be needed.

In many circles today—political, scientific, recreational—Antarctica is *in*. Some scientists say that Antarctic projects often win grant approval over similar, less expensive ones planned elsewhere. The logistics of even a small base where everything except water is imported inflates all costs wildly. For example, a 45-cent liter of aviation fuel can soar to $17 a liter—$63 a gallon—by the time it's shuttled to the interior. Yet every year finds another nation or two joining the Antarctic "club." Currently 25 countries—including Brazil, India, Peru, China, and South Korea—carry out research programs at more than 60 bases. Why do Third World debtor nations spend millions of dollars on such projects? Even a small base achieves political presence—which the nations see as a guarantee of getting their portion of resource-rich Antarctic pie, whenever it may be sliced up.

Tourists are warming to the ice continent. More than 3,200 came in the 1988-89 season. "Ten years ago," says Rothera's John Hall, "there were one or two tourist ships, making perhaps two cruises per season. Now there are a lot more. Also private yachts. And tourists are now flying in."

Of course none of this comes cheap. Luxury tour boats charge about $6,000 or more per person, double occupancy, for a two-week cruise; ten-day air tours go for almost $10,000. (Both usually begin and end at Punta Arenas, Chile, or Ushuaia, Argentina.) In 1989 a special 50-day, 750-mile ski trek across the ice cap to the South Pole carried a price tag of $79,500 for each of six customers.

While tour boats emphasize comfort, flights offer more of an outdoorsy experience, putting up passengers in tents and feeding them backpacker fare. Inevitably, they are more susceptible to Antarctica's volatile weather; one group spent eight of its ten days grounded by a whiteout on a remote island.

"A number of nations," comments Hall, "are saying, 'Well, tourists shouldn't be here.' Others are saying, 'Tourism already exists; let's try to keep a check on it so it doesn't get out of hand.'" In any emergency, nearby bases are expected to help out—and do—sidetracking their scheduled work. Personally, Hall thinks, "People have a right, if they wish to see Antarctica, to see it. But I hope it doesn't get to the level where by doing so they start to damage parts of it." The harm, he says, "would likely be unwitting, a case of sheer numbers in places that are delicate."

Ironically, Antarctica's bases, with increasingly complex needs, have affected the environment more than the tourists have. Some stations crowd the very animals they were set up to study; all pollute air and water; many trash land and ice. On occasion they are abandoned dock, stock, and barrels.

Chile's Carvajal Base—once a British outpost, on Adelaide Island—perches atop a narrow rock shore hemmed between sea and ice. Look one way and you see primeval, snowcapped mountains; turn around and you gaze on rusting oil drums, the scavenged wreck of a Single Otter aircraft that crashed years ago, and an ice cap dappled with remnants of seal meat and dog spoil. Though the British departed in 1977, these souvenirs of their dog-team operations still linger, preserved by the ice on which they lie. As a veteran of the so-called Heroic Age of the Antarctic has said, "in the deep-frozen solitudes of the last continent, Time seems to march with a lighter and slower tread. . . ." than in climates where life is sustained "by the decay of life."

Two of the heroes of exploration reached the southernmost coasts with very different attitudes and equipment. Norway's Roald Amundsen had studied the ways of the Netsilik people of the Canadian Arctic—how to manage dogs, how to coat sledge runners with thin ice so they glide over sticky snow, how to avoid exhaustion. He led his party to the South Pole, reaching it in mid-December 1911, and was safely back on the coast by January 26, 1912. Britain's pioneer, Robert Falcon Scott, relying on ponies or men to haul his sledges, found his rival's flag at the Pole on January 16; he and his party perished on the return journey. A motor sledge he had brought lies on the floor of McMurdo Sound, where rotting ice gave way under its weight. Today the United States' Amundsen-Scott base at the Pole commemorates the daring rivals, while the McMurdo base represents the era of current technology on the coast.

McMurdo, which houses as many as 1,100 people at one time, is Antarctica's largest station and has been the biggest polluter. In the 1986-87 season alone, some 8,000 tons of cargo and 5.4 million gallons of fuel went to McMurdo; only a fraction came out. For decades the station simply hauled solid wastes and scrap metal onto the winter sea ice, creating an "iron rookery" that would sink each spring. Langdon Quetin calls the underlying attitude "a World War II mentality—throw it off the road and let it sit," but finds that here and elsewhere things "have been getting better."

Nevertheless, coastal hazards take their toll. In one 30-day period of early

1989, three different ships ran aground off the Antarctic Peninsula. Argentina's *Bahia Paraíso* spilled some 160,000 gallons of diesel and other fuel only two miles from Palmer Station's important seal and seabird populations. The event was Antarctica's worst environmental injury to date. It was overshadowed almost six weeks later by another coastal casualty half a world away: the wreck of the tanker *Exxon Valdez,* which spewed millions of gallons of crude oil into Alaska's Prince William Sound.

Occurring in the summer breeding season, the *Bahia Paraíso* spill could hardly have been more ill-timed. Only days later the area's 30,000 to 35,000 penguin chicks and adults would begin their annual journey seaward. William R. Fraser of California's Point Reyes Bird Observatory saw "thousands of Adélies splashing around in intertidal pools that were almost pure diesel fuel." Diesel, he explains, is far more toxic than crude oil. "We simply don't know what the long-term impacts are going to be."

A month later a special team of scientists discovered "major effects on bird communities and intertidal areas," says Dr. Polly Penhale, a National Science Foundation program manager who headed the group. "Skuas seem to have been disoriented and didn't protect their nests; their chicks had 100 percent mortality." Cormorant chicks succumbed to internal bleeding. Limpets, the primary food of kelp gulls, also died off. Penguins apparently perished at sea, although no one knows how many.

Distressing as accidents, local disruptions, and refuse dumps may be, the most serious threats to Antarctica's shores probably stem from global side effects of civilization itself. One notorious example is the ozone "hole" that waxes and wanes seasonally above the south polar region, at times covering an area as large as the United States.

Ozone, normally a rare form of oxygen, occurs as a layer in the stratosphere; it shields the earth from some of the sun's harmful radiations, such as cancer-causing ultraviolet light, or UV. Within the past decade scientists have detected a thin spot—the hole—through which UV increasingly bombards land and sea, especially Antarctica. Ultraviolet can damage animal tissue, and too much of it can cause green plants simply to shut down. Scientists are not sure whether current UV levels endanger Antarctic phytoplankton—drifting, single-cell marine plants that feed the all-important krill. But they agree that a sharp drop in phytoplankton would set off a biological chain reaction on a worldwide scale.

They agree also on a new factor: chlorofluorocarbons, or CFCs. These man-made chemicals, widely used as propellants and refrigerants, rise to the stratosphere and interrupt the normal cycle that destroys and re-creates ozone. Many decades pass before a CFC molecule breaks down; its effects may continue even if manufacturers reduce or close out production.

Another worry, of special concern to coastal areas, is global warming. In the past century, average surface temperatures have risen about one degree Celsius. Future projections run higher: 3 to 8 degrees over the next 60 years, according to a National Academy of Sciences study. That may not seem much. But even a small change in world average temperature can drastically alter weather patterns and climates; at the height of the last ice age, some 18,000 years ago, Earth was only 10 degrees cooler. A 5-degree rise over the current average would make it warmer than at any time in the last 100,000 years.

Some scientists blame our warming trend on human activities that have swelled levels of atmospheric carbon dioxide, methane, and other "greenhouse gases." The nickname fits because, like panes of greenhouse glass, they admit solar radiation but trap some of the resultant heat. Should the "greenhouse effect" increase, marginal green areas such as North America's Great Plains or Africa's Serengeti Plain could turn to desert. And what of Antarctica's great frozen reservoir? Nobody knows. According to one widely accepted theory, a 3.5-degree increase would probably melt enough ice to raise sea level 5 or 6 feet, and the Environmental Protection Agency estimates that every foot of ocean rise translates to 100 feet of penetration inland, on average. In Florida, a 3-foot rise in sea level would flood areas as far inland as half a mile. Many of the world's most developed and populous areas lie along coastlines; devastation might be greatest in low-lying parts of China and Bangladesh.

In addition to its role in the earth's weather machinery, Antarctic ice is a record of climates past. Dusts carried in the upper atmosphere continuously settle upon the planet's surface. In major glacial areas they are preserved, filed away snowfall by snowfall, ultimately incorporated into ice. Air bubbles in the ice seal off tiny samples of atmosphere. Today's scientists can analyze these bubbles and dust records, date them, and—by comparing them—chart past climates. Perhaps they'll be able to predict future changes. They work from ice cores—vertical, continuous borings taken with a hollow drill.

Cores taken near the U.S.S.R.'s Vostok base have plumbed 2,200 meters of East Antarctic ice cap—7,220 feet, more than a mile and a quarter, and about half the distance to bedrock. They qualify as the deepest yet made. They took about ten years to drill, and represent a continuous record of some 160,000 years. They go back through the most recent ice age, when sea levels fell to expose shallows and seacoasts now hidden under water; they record the previous interglacial period, and the final centuries of an earlier glacial advance. As drill technology improves, cores may extend even farther into Antarctic ice— probing even earlier cycles of sea and shore.

Dr. Lonnie Thompson, a scientist at Ohio State University's Byrd Polar Research Center, calls such cores "an archive of Earth's environment." Isotopes of hydrogen and oxygen in a given ice sample, he explains, define past air temperatures. Dust layers reflect major dry spells, or volcanic activity like Krakatau's. Pollen grains—most common in temperate-zone, alpine glaciers—help fix plant life and climate. "We need to look at the Earth like an onion, year after year," says Thompson. "We don't understand the 'little ice age' that lowered temperatures by about a degree from 1500 through 1880 A.D.; how can we explain the big changes?" (That 'little' age was enough to doom once-flourishing Norse settlements on the coast of Greenland. Apparently their grain and hay crops failed; the livestock starved, and then the people.) Ice cores, Dr. Thompson hopes, will provide a major clue. Antarctic ice is a registry of information; in future generations, yet-unknown technologies may secure additional knowledge, knowledge and uses we may not even guess at today.

When James Cook summarized his experience off Antarctic coasts, he made some excellent guesses about their character. He considered the origin of "ice islands," the enormous tabular bergs, and deduced correctly that inland valleys would be "covered many fathoms deep with everlasting snow and at the sea they terminate in Ice clifts of vast heights." In winter, he thought, "these Ice clifts must so accumulate as to fill up all the Bays be they ever so large"—a brisk statement of how the coastline changes. At last the expanding edges of the "clifts" would break off under their own weight, to drift northward into the pack. He imagined the inland terrain: "Lands doomed by nature to everlasting frigidness . . . whose horrible and savage aspect I have no words to describe. . . ." And if someone should proceed farther south to find these lands, he concluded, "I shall not envy him the honour of the discovery but I will be bold to say that the world will not be benefited by it."

In similar vein, Lt. Charles Clerke of Cook's expedition dismissed these shores as not worth the attention "of any People under the Sun." Another prophecy proved false in our time, by 25 nations to date.

Clearly, change has come to Cook's "inaccessible" continent. Year-round bases now spatter its coasts and interior; tourists and adventurers seek its shores in season; scientists and others warn gravely of human impact even here, on the earth's final frontier. True, much of Antarctica remains pristine, tantalizingly out of reach for most people. Remoteness and weather remain primary defenses of this realm. It's not easy to imagine a resort at Cape Denison, for example, which has been called the windiest place on earth; blasts of chilled air rushing down from nearby highlands keep the average wind speed at 38 knots: 44 miles per hour, above gale force. But, though strongly defended, Antarctica is no longer *terra incognita*. Man, who once seemed so totally at Antarctica's mercy, may yet become its tyrant—though ruling more out of ignorance than design.

Early in this century, late in the epic of discovery, Scott and Amundsen proved it possible to attain the Pole. Countless others have shown we can change it, as we affect almost every other earthly place. Yes, Antarctica today is less daunting. Its bewildering coasts have been mapped, its waters charted. Its icy vastnesses are more fragile than once imagined, its awful climate and remote location no more immune to our touch than the "impenetrable tropical jungles" now being recast into grazing land and throwaway chopsticks, or the clear-cut forests of cool temperate shores. Its ice shelves may never need parkland status to forestall the spread of condos, as has occurred on milder coasts, but the take of krill and "cod" may prove as calamitous as the overfishing of anchovies off South America's littoral desert. How the earth's wild shores— even the wildest—fare in the 21st century will depend not on nature alone, but also in part on us.

FOLLOWING PAGES: Near the Antarctic Peninsula, a spectral iceberg—one of thousands—drifts northwestward past bleak shores of rock and snow.

© WOLFGANG KAEHLER

Red-coated for visibility and safety, tourists watch crabeater seals as the cruise ship World Explorer slips through sea ice toward the Antarctic Peninsula. Three thousand visitors now come annually to this land of mystery and paradox. At Deception Island—an active volcano where fumaroles pour heat into a cold bay with cinder beaches—an intrepid few test the half-mixed, steaming waters.

© WOLFGANG KAEHLER; ROBERT W. HERNANDEZ / PHOTO RESEARCHERS (ABOVE)

In the twilight below the ice, crabeater seals feed on krill—thumb-length crustaceans that swarm in the

southernmost ocean. *Overfishing and*
pollution threaten this tiny, crucial link
in the short Antarctic marine food chain.

FOLLOWING PAGES: *A strait near Cape*
Horn, with strong current and frequent
gales, once put whalers at risk.

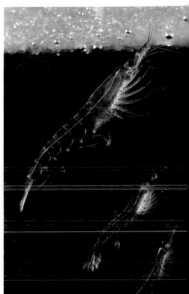

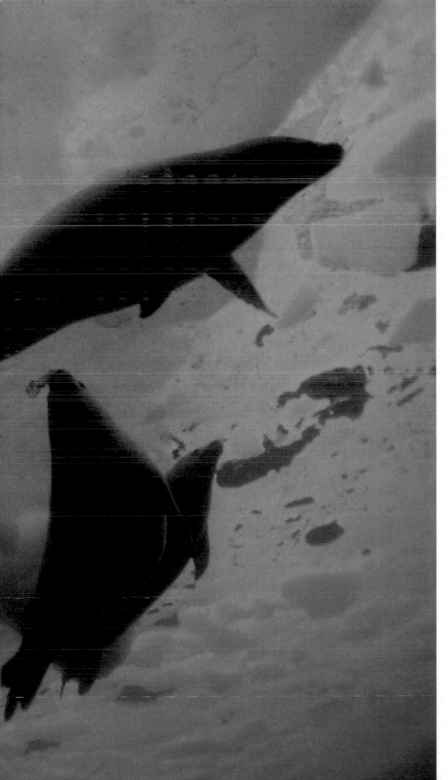

FLIP NICKLIN (ABOVE),
PAUL DRUMMOND / B & C ALEXANDER (LEFT);
M. P. KAHL / DRK PHOTO (FOLLOWING PAGES)

171

Adélie penguins lunge from a floe to find their staple: krill. Solid bones act as ballast on dives as deep as 850 feet; layers of fat, thick down, and waterproof outer feathers keep out the cold. About two feet tall, the birds can leap four times their own height or more to reach the safety of the ice and escape their chief marine predators, leopard seals.

CHRISTIANA CARVALHO (BOTH)

Already tending its own, a nesting king penguin tries to adopt an abandoned egg. Male and female kings take turns incubating one egg, held on the feet; fuzzy brown chicks take about 13 months to mature. Once hunted for their oil and plumage, kings now thrive undisturbed in rookeries on South Georgia (below) and similar islands.

FOLLOWING PAGES: *A giant berg calved from the coastal ice shelf provides "landfall" for a coterie of penguins.*

© FRANS LANTING (ABOVE); JEN AND DES BARTLETT (OPPOSITE); CHRISTIANA CARVALHO (FOLLOWING PAGES)

POLAR COASTS:

A Portfolio

The North Pole—mythical land of the midnight sun and Santa, obsession of glory-seeking explorers—has loomed larger on the horizon of civilization than its southern counterpart. Less remote than the Antarctic, which is isolated by its stormy ocean moat, the Arctic meets the populous world on the shores encircling its central sea. There, across the northern reaches of Eurasia and North America, ice gives way to treeless tundra, on a blurry frontier where the temperate realm ends and the far north begins.

The Arctic has no precise boundaries apart from the Arctic Circle—an astronomical boundary enclosing the region that sees no sunrise at the winter solstice and no sunset at the summer. Warmed in part by the North Atlantic drift, chilled elsewhere by the East Greenland and Labrador Currents, the region is a hodgepodge of microclimates determined less by latitude than by the varying influences of water, wind, and elevation.

Except on the nearly barren ice caps, life abounds here. The tundra contains grasses, sedges, lichens, wildflowers, and dwarf willows, all helping to support a richly varied fauna. Circumpolar Arctic species share their habitat with certain temperate-zone species, a legacy of the major migrations of the Pleistocene epoch. The animals, in turn, support the peoples of the Arctic. Descendants of nomadic hunters who followed the retreating ice sheets northward thousands of years ago, they learned to subsist at human limits. They found ways to thwart paralyzing wind-chill, to endure the long darkness. Their ways became the cultures of the north, passed down through the generations—and to alien visitors. By teaching explorers how to survive in the Arctic, they opened the way to both Poles. Now the modern world impinges on both polar regions, and it is their living residents who must meet new challenges in order to survive.

Preparing material for waterproof clothes and boots, an Inuit woman of the Canadian Arctic scrapes sealskin with an ulu *knife.*

JOHN EASTCOTT / YVA MOMATIUK

© JIM BRANDENBURG (BOTH)

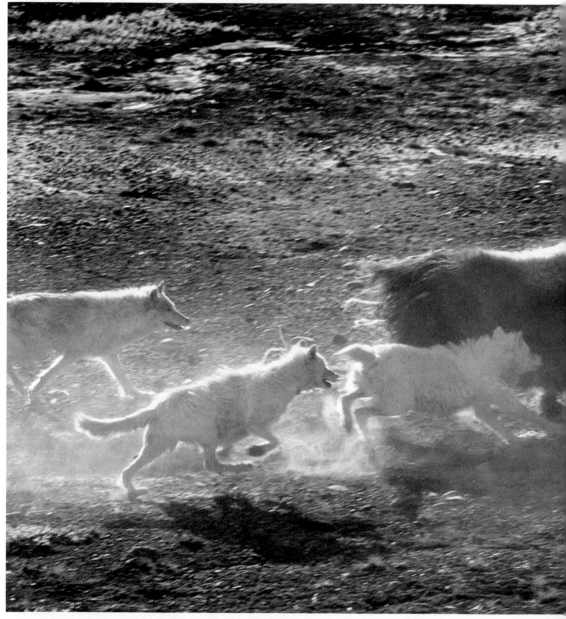

White arctic wolves run down panicking musk-oxen on Ellesmere Island. Crouched and whining, ears back, a hungry pup begs for food; a parent or other adult may respond by regurgitating half-digested meat.

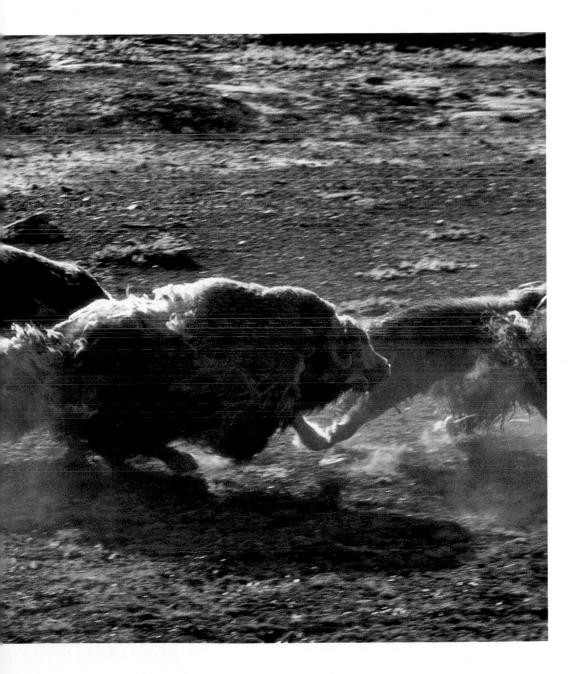

*H*unter turned scavenger in summer, a polar bear challenges Eskimo hunters for a whale carcass the humans killed the year before. Her yearling cub ignores them, tearing the rubbery flesh. Scent lured the pair from far on the skyline.

LOWELL GEORGIA

*These great predators range Arctic
shores and pack ice in quest of meat—
usually seals, in winter.*

185

Thousands of male walruses summer on the beaches of Alaska's Round Island, one of only two

© ROBERT HOLMES

"haul out" areas in the U.S. Between rest stops here, they feed at sea on marine invertebrates.

*F*ickle sunlight fosters tundra flowers on Unalaska, in Alaska's volcanic Aleutian chain. Here

the warm Kuroshio (Japan Current) enters the frigid Bering Sea, breeding fog and ferocious storms.

ART WOLFE

$\mathcal{T}$ufted puffin, often called "sea parrot" or "old man of the sea" along Alaskan and Canadian

shores, nests in coastal rock crevices and burrows. It winters at sea, in sheltered inshore waters.

KIM HEACOX

*W*orld's northernmost humans,
Eskimos of Greenland set up camp on
Inglefield Fjord in the eight-week day of
Arctic summer. Isolated in tiny villages
along the glacier-flanked 50-mile inlet,
many hunters still rely on harpoon and

BRYAN AND CHERRY ALEXANDER

kayak to take their prey—seal, walrus, and narwhal, the "sea unicorn" prized for the ivory of its single long tusk.

Instinct prompts reindeer migrations; Lapp herdsmen attend them. This herd leaves an offshore island for winter range *in northern Norway. Here, on Europe's northwestern edge, the North Atlantic Current brings water warmed in the*

distant tropics; its benisons include
the warmest summers and the longest
ice-free coast in the polar world.

© FARRELL GREHAN

© DAVID MUENCH 1988

Notes on Contributors

On assignment for Special Publications, CHRISTINE ECKSTROM has visited tropical shores around the world in the past decade. They include the Virgin Islands, French Polynesia and the Cook Islands, and the Seychelles, where she once lived for a year.

LOREN MCINTYRE, free-lance author and photographer, has contributed 15 articles to NATIONAL GEOGRAPHIC since 1966. His pictures illustrated his text in the Special Publication *The Incredible Incas and Their Timeless Land,* now in its sixth printing.

TOM MELHAM, who grew up on Long Island and takes pride in his Norwegian descent, has relished assignments to high latitudes and high elevations since 1971. He is the author of the Special Publication *John Muir's Wild America.*

A Midwesterner by birth and upbringing, THOMAS O'NEILL has turned beachcomber since writing *Back Roads America* and *Lakes, Peaks, and Prairies,* an account of the U.S.-Canadian border. He told of his ancestors' Ireland in *Majestic Island Worlds.*

As a little girl in Virginia Beach, JENNIFER C. URQUHART had "an Atlantic Ocean beach for a front yard." Washington State's Hoh River led her to the Pacific Northwest coast in coverage for a chapter in *America's Wild and Scenic Rivers.*

Additional Reading

The reader may wish to consult the *National Geographic Index* for related books and articles. In addition to books mentioned in this volume, the following may be of special interest: Rachel Carson, *The Edge of the Sea;* V. J. and D. J. Chapman, *Seaweeds and Their Uses;* Stephen Leatherwood and Randall R. Reeves, *The Sierra Club Handbook of Whales and Dolphins.*

CHAPTER 1: William H. Amos, *Wildlife of the Islands;* Archie Carr, *So Excellent a Fishe;* Robert and Barbara Decker, *Volcanoes;* Douglas Faulkner and Richard Chesher, *Living Corals;* R. E. Johannes, *Words of the Lagoon* [Palau]; David Lewis, *We, the Navigators;* Ernst Mayr, *Evolution and the Diversity of Life;* Henry and Elizabeth Stommel, *Volcano Weather.*

CHAPTER 2: Juan Antonio Fernández, *Doñana;* Wallace Kaufman and Orrin Pilkey, *The Beaches Are Moving;* Stephen P. Leatherman, *Barrier Island Handbook;* Guy Mountford, *Portrait of a Wilderness* [Doñana]; John O. Snow, *Secrets of a Salt Marsh;* Valerie Thom, *Cumberland Island / A Place Apart.*

CHAPTER 3: J. David Bowen, *The Land and People of Peru;* Mario Correa Saavedra, *Chile;* William F. Sater, *Chile and the War of the Pacific;* David P. Werlich, *Peru: A Short History.*

CHAPTER 4: Kathleen E. Dalzell, *The Queen Charlotte Islands 1774-1966;* Philip Drucker, *Cultures of the North Pacific Coast;* Tim Fitzharris, *The Island* [Vancouver Island]; Islands Protection Society, *Islands at the Edge* [the Queen Charlottes]; Robert Glenn Ketchum and Carey D. Ketchum, *The Tongass;* Eugene N. Kozloff, *Seashore Life of the Northern Pacific Coast;* Hilary Stewart, *Cedar.*

CHAPTER 5: Terence Armstrong, George Rogers, and Graham Rowley, *The Circumpolar North;* Roland Huntford, *Scott and Amundsen;* Peter Johnson, Creina Bond, and Roy Siegfried, *Antarctica;* David F. Parmelee, *Bird Island in Antarctic Waters;* Stephen J. Pyne, *The Ice;* Philip J. Quigg, *A Pole Apart;* G. Carleton Ray and M. G. McCormick-Ray, *Wildlife of the Polar Regions;* George Watson, *Birds of the Antarctic and Sub-Antarctic.*

SAMUEL H. BOARDMAN STATE PARK, OREGON

Acknowledgments

The Special Publications Division thanks the individuals and organizations named or quoted in this book, and those cited here, for their help during its preparation:

CHAPTER 1: John M. Daniels, H. Arlo Nimmo, Mrs. Yulien Rarumangkay L., Dantje T. Sembel, Raul J. Teehankee, Steven R. Walker.

CHAPTER 2: Eduardo B. Crespo, John Hall, Zachary Kirkland, Burney J. Le Boeuf, Susan Shipman.

CHAPTER 3: Allison Victor Andors, Eddie N. Bernard, David Owen Brown, Alan K. Craig, Thomas M. Davies, Jr., Vernon E. Kousky, Brian Loveman, Norbert P. Psuty, Carlos A. Salmon.

CHAPTER 4: Steve Ambrose, Guujaw, Margo Hearne, Vivian K. Hoffman, Ron Holcomb, Ron Hooper, J. Murray Mitchell, Ken Mitchell, Marla Oliver, Brian Rae, Bill Reid, Colin Richardson, Hilary Stewart, Gregory Williams.

CHAPTER 5: Paul Bogart, Bruce Manheim, Colin Monteath.

Index

Boldface indicates illustrations; *italic* refers to picture captions.

Library of Congress CIP Data

The World's wild shores / Special
Publications Division, National
Geographic Society.
    p. cm.
Includes bibliographical references.
ISBN 0-87044-716-5
ISBN 0-87044-721-1 (lib. bdg.)
    1. Coasts. I. National
Geographic Society (U.S.).
Special Publications Division.
GB451.2.W675 1990
508.314'6—dc20   89-13952   CIP

Composition by the Typographic section of National Geographic Production
Services, Pre-Press Division. Printed and bound by R. R. Donnelley & Sons,
Willard, Ohio. Color separations by Graphic Art Service, Inc., Nashville, Tenn.;
Lanman Progressive Co., Washington, D.C.; Lincoln Graphics, Inc., Cherry Hill,
N.J.; and NEC, Inc., Nashville, Tenn. Dust jacket printed by Federated
Lithographers-Printers, Inc., Providence, R.I.

NATIONAL GEOGRAPHIC SOCIETY

"For the increase and diffusion of geographic knowledge"

THE NATIONAL GEOGRAPHIC SOCIETY is chartered in Washington, D. C., as a nonprofit scientific and educational organization. Since 1890 the Society has supported more than 3,700 explorations and research projects, adding to knowledge of earth, sea, and sky.

GILBERT M. GROSVENOR, *President*
OWEN R. ANDERSON, *Executive Vice President*

Senior Vice Presidents:
ALFRED J. HAYRE, *Treasurer*
RAYMOND T. McELLIGOTT, JR.
ROBERT B. SIMS

Vice Presidents:
FREDERICK C. GALE, LEONARD J. GRANT,
JOSEPH B. HOGAN, JAMES P. KELLY,
ADRIAN L. LOFTIN, JR., LEWIS P. LOWE,
ROSS L. MULFORD, H. GREGORY PLATTS,
CLETIS PRIDE

EDWIN W. SNIDER, *Secretary*
SUZANNE DUPRÉ, *Corporate Counsel*

BOARD OF TRUSTEES

GILBERT M. GROSVENOR, *Chairman*
OWEN R. ANDERSON, *Vice Chairman*
LLOYD H. ELLIOTT, *Vice Chairman*
President, National Geographic Education Foundation

Chairmen Emeritus:
MELVIN M. PAYNE, THOMAS W. McKNEW

JOE L. ALLBRITTON
Chairman, Riggs National Bank
THOMAS E. BOLGER
Chairman, Executive Committee, Bell Atlantic
FRANK BORMAN
Chairman and CEO, Patlex Corporation
LEWIS M. BRANSCOMB
Kennedy School of Government, Harvard University
ROBERT L. BREEDEN
J. CARTER BROWN
Director, National Gallery of Art
WARREN E. BURGER
Chief Justice of the United States (Ret.)
MARTHA E. CHURCH
President, Hood College
MICHAEL COLLINS
President, Michael Collins Associates
GEORGE M. ELSEY
President Emeritus, American Red Cross
WILBUR E. GARRETT
ALFRED J. HAYRE
A. LEON HIGGINBOTHAM, JR., Judge,
U. S. Court of Appeals for the Third Circuit
JOHN JAY ISELIN
President, The Cooper Union
J. WILLARD MARRIOTT, JR.
Chairman and President, Marriott Corporation
FLORETTA DUKES McKENZIE
Former Superintendent of Schools, District of Columbia
NATHANIEL P. REED
Businessman-Environmentalist
B. FRANCIS SAUL II
President, B. F. Saul Company
ROBERT C. SEAMANS, JR.
Department of Aeronautics and Astronautics, MIT

TRUSTEES EMERITUS
CRAWFORD H. GREENEWALT, CARYL P. HASKINS,
MRS. LYNDON B. JOHNSON, CURTIS E. LeMAY,
WM. McCHESNEY MARTIN, JR., LAURANCE S.
ROCKEFELLER, FREDERICK G. VOSBURGH, JAMES H.
WAKELIN, JR., JAMES E. WEBB, CONRAD L. WIRTH

COMMITTEE FOR RESEARCH AND EXPLORATION
BARRY C. BISHOP, *Chairman;* T. DALE STEWART, *Vice Chairman;* HARM J. DE BLIJ, *Editor, National Geographic Research;* EDWIN W. SNIDER, *Secretary;* WILBUR E. GARRETT, GILBERT M. GROSVENOR, CARYL P. HASKINS, THOMAS W. McKNEW, BETTY J. MEGGERS, Research Associate-Anthropology, Smithsonian Institution, MELVIN M. PAYNE, PETER H. RAVEN, Director, Missouri Botanical Garden, CHARLES H. SOUTHWICK, Professor of Biology, University of Colorado, JOHN H. STEELE, Director, Woods Hole Oceanographic Institution, GEORGE E. STUART, JAMES H. WAKELIN, JR., GEORGE E. WATSON, FRANK C. WHITMORE, JR., Research Geologist, U. S. Geological Survey, HENRY T. WRIGHT, Professor of Anthropology, University of Michigan

NATIONAL GEOGRAPHIC MAGAZINE

GILBERT M. GROSVENOR, *President and Chairman*   WILBUR E. GARRETT, *Editor*
JOSEPH JUDGE, *Senior Associate Editor*   THOMAS R. SMITH, *Associate Editor*
CHARLES McCARRY, *Editor-at-Large*

SENIOR ASSISTANT EDITORS
THOMAS Y. CANBY, *Science* • JOHN B. GARVER, Jr., *Cartography* • WILLIAM GRAVES, *Expeditions*
NOEL GROVE, *Environment* • ROBERT W. HERNANDEZ, *Foreign Editions*
THOMAS R. KENNEDY, *Photography* • ROBERT W. MADDEN, *Layout* • SAMUEL W. MATTHEWS, *Production*
O. LOUIS MAZZATENTA, *Control Center* • ELIZABETH A. MOIZE, *Legends* • HOWARD E. PAINE, *Art*
JOHN J. PUTMAN, *Manuscripts* • LESLEY B. ROGERS, *Research* • W. ALLAN ROYCE, *Illustrations*
MARY G. SMITH, *Research Grant Projects* • GERARD A. VALERIO, *Design*

EDITORIAL
ASSISTANT EDITORS: William S. Ellis, Rowe Findley, Rick Gore, Alice J. Hall, David Jeffery, Peter Miller, Robert M. Poole, Merle Severy, Peter T. White. SENIOR WRITERS: Thomas J. Abercrombie, Harvey Arden, Mike Edwards, Bryan Hodgson, Michael E. Long, Priit J. Vesilind. SENIOR EDITORIAL STAFF: Robert Booth, Judith Brown, Charles E. Cobb, Jr., John L. Eliot, Boyd Gibbons, Larry Kohl, Douglas B. Lee, Cathy Newman, Cliff Tarpy, Jane Vessels. *Geographica:* Boris Weintraub. PRODUCTION: John L. McIntosh. EDITORIAL STAFF: Don Belt, Peter L. Porteous, Margaret N. Walsh. A. R. Williams. RESEARCH: Michaeline A. Sweeney, *Assoc. Director;* Researcher-Editors: Carolyn H. Anderson, Ann B. Henry, Jeanne E. Peters. *Researchers:* Danielle B. Beauchamp, Judith F. Bell, Victoria Cooper, Catherine C. Fox, Sheila M. Green, Jan Holderness, Anne A. Jamison, Michael Kenna, Amy E. Kezerian, Kathy B. Maher, Elizabeth R. Manierre, Barbara W. McConnell, Patricia J. Penfield, Holly Reckord, Abigail A. Tipton. *Legends:* Victoria C. Ducheneaux. *Planning Council:* Jan Hambling, Mary McPeak

ILLUSTRATIONS
PHOTOGRAPHERS: Kent J. Kobersteen, *Asst. Director;* Joseph H. Bailey, James P. Blair, Victor R. Boswell, Jr., Jodi Cobb, Bruce Dale, Emory Kristof, Joseph D. Lavenburg, George F. Mobley, James L. Stanfield; *Admin.:* Susan A. Smith, Alvin M. Chandler, Claude E. Petrone, Maria Stenzel, George Von Kantor. ILLUSTRATIONS EDITORS: William L. Allen, *Asst. Director;* David L. Arnold, William T. Douthitt, John A. Echave, Bruce A. McElfresh, Charlene Murphy, Robert S. Patton, Elie S. Rogers, Jon Schneeberger, Susan Welchman. LAYOUT: Constance H. Phelps, *Asst. Dir.;* Mary Kathryn Glassner, David Griffin. DESIGN: Betty Clayman-DeAtley, *Asst. Dir.;* Douglas M. McKenney. ART: William H. Bond, *Artist;* Karen E. Gibbs, *Research.* ENGRAVING AND PRINTING: William W. Smith, *Director;* James R. Whitney, *Assoc. Dir.;* Judy L. Garvey, John W. Gergel, Ronald E. Williamson

CARTOGRAPHY
Assoc. Directors: Allen Carroll, Alice T. M. Rechlin, John F. Shupe, Leo B. Zebarth; *Asst. Dirs.:* David P. Beddoe, John F. Dorr, Harold A. Hanson, Harry D. Kauhane, Richard K. Rogers, Elie Sabban. *Archaeologist:* George E. Stuart. *Geographer:* Ted Dachtera. *Map Editors:* Charles W. Gotthardt, Jr., *Supvr.;* John T. Blozis, Thomas L. Gray, Etelka K. Horvath, Gus Platis, Jon A. Sayre, Thomas A. Wall, Thomas A. Walsh. *Designers:* John A. Bonner, Nancy Schweickart, Sally Suominen-Summerall. *Researchers:* John L. Beeson, Dierdre T. Bevington-Attardi, Ross M. Emerson, Marguerite B. Hunsiker, Linda R. Kriete, Gretchen N. Kuhn, Gaither G. Kyhos, Mary C. Latham, David B. Miller, Dorothy A. Nicholson, Douglas A. Strobel, Juan J. Valdés, Andrew J. Wahll, Susan Young. *Text:* Oliver G.A.M. Payne. *Map Artists:* Roland R. Nichols, *Supvr.;* Iskandar Baday, James E. McClelland, Jr., Stephen P. Wells, Alfred L. Zebarth. *Computer Cartography:* Charles F. Case, Kevin P. Allen, Richard W. Bullington, Timothy J. Carter, Arthur J. Cox, Martin J. Golden, Jonathan E. Kaut. *Specialists:* Charles L. Miller, Henri A. Delanghe, Edward J. Holland

EDITORIAL SERVICES
ADMINISTRATION: M. Jean Vile, Benita M. Swash, *Assts. to the Editor;* Elaine Rice Ames, Marie L. Barnes, Mary L. Blanton, Sandra M. Dane, Lilian Davidson, Marisa Domeyko, Carol L. Dumont, Neva L. Folk, Eleanor W. Hahne, Ellen E. Kohlberg, Karen S. Marsh, Liisa Maurer, Katherine P. McGown, Susan S. Norton, Charlene S. Valeri, Ruth Winston. *Picture Requests:* Barbara A. Shattuck. *Travel:* Virginia A. Bachant, Ann C. Judge. RESOURCES: Carolyn F. Clewell, *Adm. Director; Library:* Susan Fifer Canby, *Director;* Arlene T. Drewes, Carolyn Locke, Marta Strada. *Illustrations:* Maura A. Mulvihill, *Director;* L. Fern Dame, Carolyn J. Harrison. *Records:* Mary Anne McMillen, *Director;* Ann E. Hubbs, Mennen M. Smith. *Correspondence:* Joseph M. Blanton, Jr., *Director.* *Indexes:* Jolene M. Blozis, Anne K. McCain. COMMUNICATIONS: Steve Raymer, *Director, News Service;* Kenneth C. Danforth, *Assoc. Dir.;* Joy Aschenbach, Mercer Cross, Donald J. Frederick, Robert C. Radcliffe, *Radio.* Dale A. Petroskey, *Director, Public Affairs;* Mary Jeanne Jacobsen, Barbara S. Moffet. AUDIOVISUAL: Joanne M. Hess, *Director;* Jon H. Larimore, *Tech. Dir.;* Ronald S. Altemus, Scott A. Brader, Robert G. Fleegal, Paul Gorski, P. Andrew van Duym, Gerald L. Wiley

ADMINISTRATION
ASST. VICE PRESIDENTS: Joyce W. Graves, *Asst. to the President;* Robert G. Corey, Thomas E. Kulikosky, Carol E. Lang, Carl M. Shrader, Paul B. Tylor. ASST. TREASURER: Dorothy M. Wagner. GEOGRAPHIC LIAISON: Barry C. Bishop. ASSTS. TO THE PRESIDENT: Richard E. Pearson, *Diplomatic and Civic Affairs;* Robert E. Dulli, *Education.* ACCOUNTING: Dorothy J. Edwards, Douglas E. Hill, Laura L. Leight, George E. Newstedt. ADMINISTRATION: Margaret R. Herndon, Robert V. Koenig, Zbigniew Jan Lutyk, Marta M. Marschalko, Myra A. McLellan, Jennifer Moseley, Janet C. Newell, Jimmie D. Pridemore, Joyce S. Sanford, Myla Stewart, Frank M. Twigger. COMPUTER: Scott Bolden, Warren Burger, William L. Chewning, George F. Hubbs, Ronald C. Kline, Richard A. Mechler, James G. Schmelzer, Harold E. Smith. EDUCATIONAL SERVICES: Wendy G. Rogers, Dean R. Gage, Carl W. Harmon, Jr., Albert Meyer. EXPLORERS HALL: Jeffrey A. Dering. MEMBERSHIP SERVICES: Margaret L. Bassford, Robert C. Dove, Carol A. Houck, Marguerite M. Wise, Peter F. Woods. PERSONNEL: Robert E. Howell, Glenn G. Pepperman, Shirley N. Wilson. PROMOTION: Joseph S. Fowler, Joan Anderson, James R. Dimond, Jr., Robert L. Feige, Deborah A. Jones, Charles T. Kneeland, Lucy J. Lowenthal, F. William Rath. PURCHASING: Margaret Cole, Thomas L. Fletcher

PRODUCTION SERVICES
QUALITY: Frank S. Oliverio, Bill M. Aldridge. PRE-PRESS: Geoffrey T. McConnell, Billy R. Barnett, Richard A. Bredeck, David H. Chisman, Phillip E. Plude, Bernard G. Quarrick. PHOTOGRAPHIC LAB: William S. Petrini, James H. Trott, Alfred M. Yee. PRINTING: Hans H. Wegner, Joseph M. Anderson, Sherrie S. Harrison. ADMINISTRATION: Lawrence F. Ludwig, *Director;* Joan S. Simms

ADVERTISING
George E. Moffat, *Vice President.* Joan McCraw, *National Director.* James D. Shepherd, *Western Manager.* O. W. Jones, Jr., *Detroit Manager.* Robert D. Johnson, *Los Angeles Manager.* Debra J. Grady, *New York Manager.* Laurie L. Kutsche, *Chicago Manager.* Philip G. Reynolds, *Special Accounts Manager.* Michel A. Boutin, *International Director,* 90, Champs-Élysées, 75008 Paris. *Washington:* Alex MacRae, *Marketing/Sales.* Pandora Browne, *Promotion.* Sarita L. Moffat, *Operations.* Renee S. Clepper, *Research.* Gail M. Jackson, *Production*

TELEVISION
Tim T. Kelly, *Vice President and Director;* Yeorgos N. Lampathakis, Marjorie M. Moomey, Nola L. Shrewsbery, Kathleen F. Teter

EDUCATIONAL SERVICES OF THE SOCIETY
ROBERT L. BREEDEN, *Senior Vice President*

Danforth P. Fales, *Vice President;* William R. Gray, *Exec. Asst.;* Suzanne J. Jacobson, *Asst. to the Sr. Vice Pres.;* Stephen J. Hubbard, Carolyn W. Jones, Betsy Ellison. BOOK SERVICE: Charles O. Hyman, *Director and Sr. Asst. Editor;* Ross Bennett, *Assoc. Dir.;* David M. Seager, *Art Dir.;* Greta Arnold, Mary Dickinson, John T. Dunn, Susan C. Eckert, Karen F. Edwards, Charlotte Golin, J. Edward Lanouette, Linda B. Meyerriecks, Elizabeth Newhouse, M. Patt-Corner, David F. Robinson, Margaret Sedeen, Jean K. Teichroew, Penelope Timbers, Jonathan Tourtellot, Richard Wain. SPECIAL PUBLICATIONS: Donald J. Crump, *Director and Sr. Asst. Editor;* Philip B. Silcott, *Assoc. Dir.;* Bonnie S. Lawrence, *Asst. Dir.;* Jody Bolt, *Art Dir.;* John G. Agnone, Jane H. Buxton, Margery G. Dunn, Toni Eugene, David V. Evans, Ron Fisher, Patricia F. Frakes, Mary Ann Harrell, Charles E. Herron, Alice Jablonsky, Jane R. McCauley, Tom Melham, Robert Messer, H. Robert Morrison, Thomas O'Neill, Barbara A. Payne, Thomas B. Powell III, Cynthia Ramsay, Cinda Rose, David V. Showers, Viviane Y. Silverman, Gene S. Stuart, Jennifer C. Urquhart, George V. White. WORLD: Pat Robbins, *Editor;* Margaret McKelway, *Assoc. Editor;* Ursula Vosseler, *Art Dir.;* Jacqueline Geschickter, Pat Holland, Veronica Morrison, Judith Rinard, Eleanor Shannahan. EDUCATIONAL MEDIA: George A. Peterson, *Director;* Jimmie Abercrombie, Julie V. Agnone, David Beacom, Monica P. Bradsher, James B. Caffrey, Betty G. Kotcher, Sandra L. Matthews, Louise C. Millikan. TRAVELER: Richard Busch, *Editorial Dir.;* Paul Martin, *Editor;* Suez B. Kehl, *Art Dir.* PUBLICATIONS ART: John D. Garst, Jr., *Director;* Virginia L. Baza, *Assoc. Dir.;* Isaac Ortiz, *Asst. Dir.;* Peter J. Balch. EDUCATIONAL FILMS: Sidney Platt, *Director;* Donald M. Cooper, *Assoc. Dir.;* Suzanne K. Poole, Carl E. Ziebe

---

NATIONAL GEOGRAPHIC magazine makes an ideal gift for any occasion. For information about membership in the National Geographic Society, call 800-638-4077, toll free, or write to the National Geographic Society, Dept. 1675, Washington, D. C. 20036.